THIS BOOK BELONGS TO
The Library of

....

....

@COPYRIGHT 2024

The content contained within this book may not be reproduced, duplicated, or transmitted without direct written permission from the author or the publisher. Under no circumstances will any blame or legal responsibility be held against the publisher, or author, for any damages, reparation, or monetary loss due to the information contained within this book. Either directly or indirectly.

Legal Notice:

This book is copyright protected. This book is only for personal use. You cannot amend, distribute, sell, use, quote, or paraphrase any part, or the content within this book, without the consent of the author or publisher.

Disclaimer Notice:

Please note the information contained within this document is for educational and entertainment purposes only. All effort has been executed to present accurate, up-to-date, and reliable, complete information. No warranties of any kind are declared or implied. Readers acknowledge that the author is not engaging in the rendering of legal, financial, medical, or professional advice. The content within this book has been derived from various sources. Please consult a licensed professional before attempting any techniques outlined in this book. By reading this document, the reader agrees that under no circumstances is the author responsible for any losses, direct or indirect, which are incurred as a result of the use of the information contained within this document, including, but not limited to — errors, omissions, or inaccuracies.

Did you like my book? I pondered it severely before releasing this book. Although the response has been overwhelming, it is always pleasing to see, read or hear a new comment. Thank you for reading this and I would love to hear your honest opinion about it. Furthermore, many people are searching for a unique book, and your feedback will help me gather the right books for my reading audience.

Thanks!

Table of Contents

Introduction	5
Chapter 1: The Essential Guide to Social Media Marketing	8
Chapter 2: Growing Your Brand and Your Business with Great Content	56
Chapter 3: Marketing on Twitter and Using the Platform as a Gateway to Other Social Channels	105
Chapter 4: YouTube for Marketing and as a Passive Income Generator	141
Chapter 5: Instagram for Marketing People and Businesses	156
Chapter 6: TikTok Marketing 101	190
Chapter 7: The Ultimate Guide to Twitch Marketing	203
Conclusion	213

INTRODUCTION

Businesses, in today's day and age, are largely dominated by the customers and their demands. SMM, short for social media marketing, is a necessity for increasing revenues and for improving a brand's reach. Both freelancers and corporate marketers employ social media marketing (SMM) to find clients and fulfill their marketing objectives.

Improving web traffic, increasing view counts, and generating huge profits are just some of the benefits of social media marketing. In the digital world, a decent number of followers can translate to high earnings. On average, social media marketers earn five to six figures annually. Internet icons, like influencers, YouTubers, streamers, and affiliates, can make six to seven figures per month.

With an account on one of the top social channels on the web, nothing is impossible for you. All you need is at least a thousand followers. From there, you can opt to be a freelancer, podcaster, or affiliate. By offering high-quality content, you have the chance to be a well-known internet icon, who receives payment and freebies in exchange for promotional content.

Social media marketing has expanded many careers as well. Today, digital marketers can target high-paying positions. Associates can become specialists, directors, coordinators, and operations managers. Social media is a powerful channel of marketing, serving as a game-changer for many entities. The industry is expanding, and so too are the number of opportunities to earn online.

This book "Mastering Social Media Algorithm" aims to introduce the world of social media marketing (SMM), in an easy-to-digest way. In each chapter, a new social platform is introduced, and brand-new ways to establish passive income are detailed. What's more, you can finally learn how to easily grow your followers and subscribers, as well as learn the following marketing essentials:

✓ The fundamentals of social media marketing (SMM)
✓ Outsmarting social media algorithms to your advantage
✓ Combining social media marketing (SMM) and search engine optimization (SEO) for better results
✓ Gaining traction on search engines with social channels
✓ Identifying marketing goals and defining target audiences
✓ Creating a buyer persona
✓ Why YouTube is the best social media platform
✓ Getting paid by partnership programs
✓ Becoming an affiliate and influencer on the top social platforms
✓ Using tone effectively in branding
✓ Tracking campaigns and setting up paid and organic campaigns
✓ Making money on Instagram

These topics are just the tip of the iceberg. When you reach Chapters 2 and 3, you can learn how to win the hearts of prospects with words. The proper way of communication is one of the essential keys in social media marketing (SMM), and that's just one of them that has been expounded in this book. There are many more!

Thank you so much for downloading this book! I hope you enjoy it.

CHAPTER 1: THE ESSENTIAL GUIDE TO SOCIAL MEDIA MARKETING

Social media platforms, including Twitter, Facebook, and Youtube, provides a variety of marketing opportunities. They offer a collection of online services facilitating 2-way communication and web content sharing. The digital content can include digital media, formatted texts, and peer-to-peer (P2P) documents.

For marketers, social media is a valuable tool when growing businesses, improving brand exposure, and selling products and services. For prospects and leads, which include viewers, buyers, followers, etc., social networking platforms serve as their gateway to the world, enabling them to look up people, services, and places, with just a few mouse clicks.

Social media can indeed become a productive component of your marketing strategies. Enhancing business visibility, creating rapport with leads, and expanding other forms of marketing, SMM, or social media marketing, has taken the marketing industry and the digital world by storm.

Over the years, it has undeniably defeated conventional advertising methods, like word-by-mouth, door-to-door selling, and network marketing. What's the reason for this?

Day by day, thousands of new users register on social networking services (SNS). To date, the top three SNS platforms for digital marketing are Facebook, Youtube, and Instagram. This is according to Forbes, a world-renowned and well-refuted American business magazine.

Facebook, alone, has 2.3 billion active users. It's followed by YouTube with 1.9 billion monetizable leads. Instagram, Facebook's sister company, ranks 3rd. Meanwhile, Twitter remains the top SNS in Japan and other countries, with 330 million daily active users. Even in 4th place, Twitter has approximately 70 million unique American users.

What's more, other budding SNS websites have experienced a massive rise in registrations and daily logins in the last two years. Among the ranks include TikTok, Twitch, and Pinterest. With the rise of IoT devices and the digital age, many are entering the online world for their convenience, entertainment, and necessities, whether it be for basic, personal, or professional purposes.

The Temptation of SMM

With the exponential rise of social media users, SMM sounds tempting especially if you've a business or you're planning to establish one. Often, SMM as a marketing tool requires zero cash.

Yes, there are paid services and advertising options, but if you go all organic, you won't need any amount of capital. You just need the right knowledge and skills. If you do SMM right, you'll see that customers will flood to your cyber door days after you've launched your page, account, or website.

Both the marketing and social media industry are vast. That's why your journey to mastering social marketing will be a step-by-step process. The first chapter of this book is here to introduce you to a whole new world of SNS, marketing, digital analytics, and passive income.

Defining Social Media Marketing?

In general, the term social media marketing refers to online strategies and services that greatly emphasize relationship selling. Why do you use social media? Aside from connecting with your family and friends, you may have also viewed it as a medium for growing your business. You're not wrong!

Fundamentally, social media marketing is a form of digital marketing. It involves sharing and creating digital content on websites and SNS apps to achieve branding marketing goals, which include, but are not limited to the following:

- ✓ Increase engagement and web traffic
- ✓ Improve brand exposure and lead conversion rates
- ✓ Build email listings and reach prospects in other countries
- ✓ Increase sales and profits
- ✓ Gain viewers, followers, and subscribers
- ✓ Drive click-throughs on paid advertisements
- ✓ Enter new niches, markets, and communities

At its core, SMM has six foundations. To give you a headstart, here are the main foundations of social media marketing.

- ✓ Strategy
- ✓ Planning and publishing
- ✓ Engagement and listening
- ✓ Data and marketing analytics
- ✓ Content creation
- ✓ Paid and organic advertising

You can learn more about each of the steps in the next sections. Marketing of this form encompasses traditional free online publishings of media and texts. These are then tweaked in order to achieve set goals, like the ones listed above.

The phrase generally refers to the use of such online services for developing rapport and relationship selling. Take a freelance artist for example. Beginner artists on IG and Twitter often start with zero followers. Their first new followers may just be their friends and relatives.

As they create content and actively participate in clusters and groups, they build relationships with people who're interested in what they can offer. In this case, they offer art! They will follow those people in the hopes of having mutuals. This can pave the way for more opportunities.

Depending on the platform, mutuals can offer new free leads. Please keep in mind that the word "leads' has many meanings. In marketing, leads could be a buyer, searcher, or follower. As a rule of thumb, a lead is any person or user who is looking for something on the web. Lead generation is the process of making people fulfill set goals, such as the following:

- ✓ Making a purchase
- ✓ Liking or sharing a post
- ✓ Clicking the "Subscribe" button
- ✓ Commenting or retweeting
- ✓ Availing of a service

Going back on topic, artists can benefit from the followers of their "mutuals." Even if you only have a few hundred followers, but your friend has 3,000, then you can consider them as your leads as well.

For example, Twitter offers 100% organic impressions for all online leads. This means that all of your friend's online followers can see your posts as well. However, this is only possible if that "friend" engages with your content. In SMM, engagement includes likes, shares, clicks, and comments.

By engaging followers and responding to their responses and supporting their page/SNS account, you're building trust and creating rapport. Artists, in particular, often collaborate with their fellow artists in order to increase their audience and improve brand exposure. In the process, they attract possible clients who are willing to commission them for what they make.

Social media marketing employs online technologies and innovative services to achieve familiar communication and fulfills marketing goals. The tried-and-tested marketing strategies, like answering inquiries and solving customer problems, serve as the heart of some advertising campaigns. This topic is expounded in chapter 2 and 4.

This book "Mastering Social Media Algorithms" is a comprehensive guide to the world of SMM. It can help you master social networking algorithms, as well as become a marketing expert in the top social channels on the web.

-Taking a Closer Look at the Benefits

SMM offers a great many benefits. With this type of digital marketing, you can grow your brand, increase sales, and reach new prospects for free. SMM is an option for free--zero-cost--marketing.

Every day, a myriad of people is on social networking sites. By Q2 2016, Facebook claimed that they have 2 billion monthly active users worldwide. Approximately, 85% of the social media giant's web traffic is from outside the USA and Canada.

If you compare FB to Google, this social media behemoth is in close competition with the search engine giant. In October of the same year, Facebook recorded over 200 million unique US viewers/visitors. Of course, visitors do different things on the two online giants.

Twitter also tallied 109 million active users in October 2016. That figure is just their unique viewers/visitors in the United States. In that month, they have totaled 500 million active users and experienced 400 million daily tweets.

Even focused social networking websites, like Twitch and TikTok, have recently experienced a spike in their daily visitors. They have hundreds of millions of active users per day.

All of the said facts and statistics imply that there are a lot of prospects and marketing opportunities on the top social networking platforms.

What are the Different Types of Careers on social media?

Today, social media career opportunities are increasing, and there's nothing stopping them. Every day, someone needs a new SMM specialist or content manager. Facebook advertising, one of the most lucrative forms of marketing, needs specific skillsets like sales funneling and digital analytics.

Search engines are changing and so too are social media platforms. Many times, a year, YouTube and Instagram introduce something new, and their search algorithms are upgraded or modified.

Local businesses around the world are turning to SNS websites, like Twitter and Instagram, to improve their sales and increase the number of their loyal customers. On YouTube, millions of users watch videos to be entertained or to know something.

The facts are there. There are over 300 million monthly active users on Twitter. Approximately, 5 billion videos are watched on YouTube every day. Instagram, the sister company of Facebook, has 500 million daily active users.

What do these facts imply? Businesses, including start-ups and well-rooted organizations, need people to handle all the data, all the marketing and sales processes, and all the users who engage with their brands online. All of these tasks create job opportunities:

- ☐ Content Manager
- ☐ Digital Media Supervisor
- ☐ Digital Marketing Manager
- ☐ Social Media Specialist
- ☐ Online Community Manager
- ☐ Engagement Coordinator
- ☐ SMM Analyst
- ☐ Public Relations Manager
- ☐ SMM Manager
- ☐ Brand Advocate
- ☐ Online Communications Director
- ☐ SMM Strategist
- ☐ Brand Manager

-What are the Progression Opportunities for a Career in social media?

Seasoned social media specialists and other professionals in the digital marketing industry can seek management-level positions. Some of these experienced experts might have also work in other areas of marketing, which include digital analytics, video production, copywriting, and design/graphics. This is they can pursue management-level positions in digital marketing.

SMM and SEO

As technology develops, the algorithms of search engines and web crawlers evolve as well. Search engine bots or web crawlers are programs that scan online content for search engine ranking.

Today, they've gotten more complex and smarter than they were 5 years ago. Plus, the markets that use the web for growth ad exposure are extremely saturated. This means that there could be intense competition in your industry.

The founder and SEO consultant of Rank Tree, Hunter Branch, has observed firsthand what good SEO can do for brand exposure. He said, "For some businesses, SEO can help in improving engagement and brand awareness by 70 to 90 percent. With search engine optimization, the name and logo of your business could show up in three of the world's most popular search engines, namely Google, Yahoo, and Bing."

For most people, SEO is just an afterthought, but even Google, the largest search engine in the world that accounts for 90 to 95 percent of all the daily searches on the internet, advises that startups must implement SEO early, rather than later.

When you're launching a new website or social media page, do incorporate search engine optimization in web development and content management. Before publishing content, incorporate SEO in writing and editing.

-SEO in Marketing

Search engine optimization shouldn't just be a topping on your marketing strategies. Rather, you must let it take root or become the base ingredient. This applies when you're growing your brand too. According to Neil Patel, one of the most successful digital marketers in the 21st century, Google and its crawlers greatly considers the following when generating search engine results pages (SERP):

- ✓ Website speed
- ✓ User-friendliness
- ✓ Content marketing
- ✓ Keywords
- ✓ High quality digital content
- ✓ Site design
- ✓ Search intent

Search engine optimization influences many aspects of a website or social media page. No matter in whatever niche or industry you're in, the quality of the content you offer online and how it's "optimized" can affect the future success or downfall of your business.

-What Needs to be Done?

According to Forbes, managing your business's online reputation and presence is integral to improving sales. Bad or good, things get spread fast online. Many consumers, especially those that patronize trends, rely on online research before making a purchase or availing of a service.

That's the main reason why SEO should serve as the base ingredient in your brand management plans. SEO can be used in many fields and industries and it's the fastest way to leverage your busieness's exposure online. With the right optimization, your website or social media page could experience an influx of web traffic overnight.

So, what needs to be done? The answers to that question are "professional content and website optimization" and "cost-efficient link building, keyword research, and social media integration."

- ☐ Link Building

The total number of "quality" inbound links correlates with a higher SERP ranking. SERP stands for search engine results page. The links and meta titles of the web pages served to searchers after they enter a query, word, or phrase are included in SERP.

The user in question enters the query, which is often composed of phrases called keywords. Then, the search engine generates a list. This list is what you call SERP. Keywords have two types: short-tail and long-tail.

The higher you're in SERP, the more visitors your website or social media gets. The more "quality" inbound links your content have, the higher your rank will be. However, this is only possible if you meet the other criteria. These are discussed in the next sections.

☐ Optimizing Keyword Phrases

Like link building, keyword research and content optimization can also boost organic traffic. The term "organic marketing" refers to any strategy that generates traffic to online businesses without employing sponsorship or paid ad services.

Any form of zero-cost brand promotion is under organic marketing. According to Marilyn Wilkinson, a copywriter and digital marketer at Full Stack Copywriter, organic visibility, on the major search engines and social media in the world, is integral for reaching set marketing goals and for boosting brand awareness KPI.

Marilyn says, "If you're not incorporating SEO in your marketing campaigns, you're leaving the door open for your rivals to steal customers and prospects right under your nose."

Neil Patel, Dan Lok, and Marilyn Wilkinson use keyword optimization in their marketing and copywriting endeavors. Using keywords in the introduction and some subheadings is just one effective practice.

☐ Integrate Social Media Channels with SEO

Another option aside from organic marketing is "the integration of web content with other marketing channels." These include social media platforms and video-sharing sites.

The combination of search engine optimization and social media marketing is a match made in heaven in terms of creating rapport, connecting with prospects, and improving brand exposure.

What's more, content on social networking sites gets indexed by crawlers as well. Particularly, the descriptions in YouTube videos and tweets with hashtags are well-loved by the search spiders.

Just make sure that your content stays relevant with the keywords you're using. Otherwise, indexing will not happen. If you do choose to utilize social media marketing in influencing SEO results, then you must consider the future path of your company and implement professional SEO solutions that can benefit you in the long run.

Leveraging Search Engine Optimization (SEO) for Improved Visibility

Regardless of how popular Facebook, Twitter, and YouTube have become, SEO will remain the most important cybersocial toolkit for your brand's overall web presence.

The goal of search engine optimization is to leverage the components of your digital content in SERP's top ten. If your page or profile doesn't end up in SERP's top ten, then your competitors will beat you when it comes to web traffic.

In digital marketing, the higher your web traffic is, the more sales and leads you'll generate. Remember, even social media profiles get indexed by search engines. Even Duck Duck Go factors keywords in dishing out their search results.

According to SproutSocial, only 26% of searchers browse the 2nd and 3rd pages of every search engine results page. 70% of internet surfers only click on the first page. Without SEO, you'll miss a lot of marketing opportunities.

-Getting Started

Basically, you can optimize your online content by incorporating keywords or search terms and then leveraging the following:

- ✓ Page structure
- ✓ Online profiles
- ✓ Ease of use
- ✓ Images and video files
- ✓ Navigation
- ✓ Blog posts and other digital content

At the same time, you also need to maximize cross-links from other social media profiles. You need to do all these to increase the number of inbound links to your account and pages.

In this section, you can learn more about the following:

- ✓ Use the top search engines (e.g, Bing, Google, and Yahoo) for SMM
- ✓ Integrate SEO fundamentals, like using metatags and keywords, into your marketing plan
- ✓ Why search engine optimization still matters today
- ✓ Optimize your social media profile for search engines and web searchers

-Thinking Practically and Tactically

SEO is a form of organic internet marketing. These are marketing methods that do not require paid advertisements, except if the marketer opts to pay for the services of an influencer.

High-quality content brings forth the best results for SEO. This fact also remains true for enticing prospects. No one will believe you that you're selling a high-quality micro-SD card when there are typographical errors in its packaging. If they see "watel-proof," instead of "water-proof," then prospective buyers will turn away from your product.

SEO revolves around that fact and other technicalities, like user-friendliness and proper wording. When it comes to social media marketing, some schools of thought drive optimization tactics:

✓ Website leveraging

✓ Usage of search terms

✓ Attaining a top rank with one or more social media post relevant to your niche

✓ Using social media pages to attain a high rank in SERP

-Search Engine Jargons

Before you dive into the tastiest part of this section, please acquaint yourself with some integral terms in search engine optimization. You'll often see them pop up from time to time wherever this topic is tackled.

☐ Meta-titles

The pages that appear in SERP's top ten have optimized titles, which include a keyword or two. Meta titles are those that you see on the first results pages. They're clickable and will redirect you to the source of the content.

☐ Paid search results

Paid search results are advertised on web pages. The creator of the advertised web page has paid a bid or submission fee to appear at the top of the results for specific keywords. Even on Google or Bing, paid content could include a blog or social media post.

However, paid search results don't appear on the web browsers of users who've installed an ad-blocking add-on.

☐ Search engine marketing

Search engine marketing, or SEM, combines forms of both paid and organic internet marketing. Together with SMM, SEM can bear profitable results.

☐ Social media optimization

SMO stands for social media optimization. Like Google and Duck Duck Go, SNS websites also provide a search function, wherein you can search for other users, places, groups, hashtags, and keywords. Leveraging your content for social media searches is the basis of SMO.

How a post/tweet/video ranks on such search results depends on the social media platform. This will be greatly discussed in the following chapters. The search algorithm on YouTube is different on Facebook and Instagram.

☐ Web crawlers

Web crawlers have many names, including the following:

-Spiders

-Robots

-Search bots

-Google bots

-Bing bots

-Crawlers

In general, web crawlers are automated programs, which function like AI. Their behavior and how they rank posts and web pages depend on set algorithms.

These algorithms remain fixed, unless a modification or update is applied to them.

-The Top Search Engines to Consider

Google has unique algorithms. Often, this search engine giant introduces updates and revisions every quarter. On the other hand, Bing and Yahoo share identical search rules. Many Windows 10 users utilize Bing as their primary search engine.

In June 2020, ComScore reported that the top three search engines, which are Google, Bing, and Yahoo, accounts for 97% of all searches on the Web. Google executes three times as many searches as Bing. The remaining search engines, including MSN and Duck Duck Go, account for the remaining 3%.

That's why it's essential to resubmit routinely. This is especially true if you're using a form of paid advertising. On your social media profiles, make it a habit to update existing content and do publish regularly.

By doing so, you'll trigger visitations from the web crawlers. Adding fresh and optimized digital content makes the arachnid bots rank new product pages.

To reiterate, different search engines and social media platforms use different sets of rules for displaying search results. Also, they attract various groups of people. For example, 75% of Twitter users belong to the working class, and 56% of Instagram users are aged between 15 and 35.

That's why you must optimize your websites and social media profiles for the search engine that attracts your brand's prospects.

Here are some basic facts about Google, Yahoo, and Bing that an upstart marketer should take note of. These can benefit your SEO efforts, posting schedules, and digital advertising tactics.

- ☐ If you compare Google users to the overall population of web surfers, there are more males than females. On the one hand, Bing and Yahoo users are mainly comprised of females.
- ☐ Most Millennials prefer Google over other search engines. Those who are over 35 tend to use Bing and Yahoo.
- ☐ According to SproutSocial, the majority of Google users surf the web during work hours Monday to Friday.
- ☐ In contrast, Bing and Yahoo users are considered morning doves. They're most active in the wee hours of the morning till 7 am.
- ☐ Due to the popularity of Android phones, Google tops mobile searches. Most Apple users, on the one hand, prefer Bing or Yahoo.
- ☐ Google's competitors—Bing and Yahoo--are popular on households with over $75,000 annual household income.

-The Significance of Knowing the Right Search Phrases

Surfers enter keywords in the search box on a directory, search engine, or SNS website to find the data they seek. The key to social media SEO and organic search engine marketing is knowing the hashtags and search terms that your prospects use.

To improve visibility on any social media platform, your social media profile or page needs to appear in the top ten of the results pages. The top ten URLs are generated on the first page. Casual surfers don't search past the first page; only researchers and people with OCD do.

Unfortunately, or fortunately, everyone has a different brain makeup. No two individuals are the same. For this reason, some use different word choices and others organize words differently. Some subtle differences could be due to dialect and native language.

For example, those in the wild west will search for "buckets." In contrast, internet surfers originating in North Carolina will use "pail" when searching for such a product on the web. Brits will enter "cheap petrol," while Americans will search for "cheap gas."

Here are some more key points before you head to the next section. You should use them whenever you're "researching for keywords." Keyword research and other SEO essentials are detailed in the following sections.

☐ The average length of a query for English users, including those who learned English as a secondary language, is between two and three words.

☐ With location-based and personal searches, most everyday surfers only enter very few words.

☐ Long search queries are often questions, like the following:

-How to take care of your cat?

-What are the symptoms of canine distemper?

-How to make $100 daily on Twitter?

☐ Further, mobile users nowadays employ Voice Search when looking for the answer to a practical question, such as:

-What are the basic ingredients of cheesecake?

-Where can I buy cheap petrol in London?

-The top five cat breeds in America

- Longer keywords are search queries composed of four or more words.

When researching keywords and considering several of them, avoid limiting your choices to the top search terms for your topic. You must also take note of the words and phrases your prospects might use for searching for what they need online. That's the major purpose of keyword research.

Keyword Research for Social Media Marketing

As a marketer, you need to research first before posting anything on your SNS profile. For the sake of your brand and so that your marketing efforts will bear good results, you must leverage and optimize each social media post you'll publish. This involves the use of SEO and keyword research.

Although SEO may sound time-consuming, it will be easy to implement once you've gotten the hang of it.

Firstly, come up with thirty search queries. Now, how can you be sure that all of them are relevant? Just follow the tips below:

- Use a keyword research tool, like Soovle and Google's Keyword Research Planner.

- Brainstorm all the possible words your prospects may use. You should ask your employees and loyal customers for this. In the next chapters, you'll learn how to easily interact with your followers and how to ask the right questions.

- You can include the name and type of your service or product in the list. You can also include your company's name, but you shouldn't prioritize it above the other search terms.

- This is very important. Include all jargon and industry-specific terms.

- [ ] If you're catering to the residents of a specific region or local territory, you must include the location in your choices. For example, if your commercial bakery is located in Los Angeles, use the search queries "tasty bakery LA" or "pastries bakery LA."
- [ ] One word is not enough to land you on the first page, but a combination of words or the incorporation of various types of keywords into your content will do.
- [ ] There are free tools online for keyword research like SEMRush and Google Keywords Planner.
- [ ] Google can also come in handy. Enter a possible search query and tap the Search button. After this, click the Related Searches option located in the page's left margin. You can find the top search phrases there.
- [ ] One of the best ways to know the best keywords for your content is to check your top competitor's keywords. Then, you need to confirm the efficacy of the search terms using a keyword research tool.
- [ ] To find the keywords used in any web page, open your browser's toolbar and look for the "View Source" section and click that. The keywords are listed at the top or the bottom of the codes.
- [ ] Another way is to use the "Find command" tool. To execute it, press the CTRL and F buttons simultaneously. A search box will pop up at the top of the web page. Type into its "keyword" and press Enter.
- [ ] To know who's your top competitors, search on Google, Yahoo, or Bing the most relevant keyword to your content. The first ten results on SERP's 1st page are your top rivals.

☐ Tag clouds help you visualize the frequency of the appearance of a keyword in content. You can also use blog search engines like IceRocket for assessing the popularity of a keyword.

Building a social media profile and using four to five search terms can be difficult. That's why it's best to divide your terms list into specific sets and only use the most effective ones.

-Where to Use the Keywords

Foremost, you need to use two or more keywords in your profile bio. And, sprinkle, sparingly, the keywords throughout your other social media content. If your old posts are relevant, you may edit some of them. However, not all SNS platforms allow editing of past posts.

Google bots also scour social media pages and profiles. That's why it's necessary to include search terms in your bio, tagline, and pinned post. Do include four to five keywords per page and heading. You can also introduce new keywords in fresh content. Only do this if they're frequently used.

Aim for a 2% to 5% keyword density. That's why the longer your post is, the more keywords you can include. But please avoid posting long-form articles and content with more than 3,000 characters. If you have to, link a URL containing the article in a post instead.

On Twitter and other micro-blogging websites, the keyword density should only be one to three percent. If there are too many keywords, both users and crawlers will turn away away from the post.

Remember, internet surfers and web crawlers dislike walls of texts. So, be clear and concise and choose your words well. Avoid writing fluff and only include what's necessary.

-Metatags: What You Need to Know

Search engines, as well as their crawlers, use descriptions and title metatags when ranking a blog, web page, or social media post. It was different in the past--some twenty-plus years ago.

Today, search engines only need the description and meta title of a page to categorize and rank its content. Hence, you must include keywords in the meta title and meta tag of your post.

Page and description tags are now important to social media marketing. Facebook, Pinterest, YouTube, and other SNS websites pull content from such tags when the URL is retweeted or shared.

Metatags, hashtags, and normal tags are different from each other. Metatags refer to entries (search terms) appearing in page source codes that have the term "tags."

Therefore, a metatag can be considered a type of keyword. Hashtags, on the other hand, are for tagging and categorization, but they also function as keywords. On Twitter and Pinterest, if you include a hashtag in your post that has an image, that image can appear on Google's photo section or the first page of SERP.

Here are some valuable tips for using metatags:

- If a marketable web page has no page description or meta title, it will likely not end up in the top ten list.

- Use <alt> tags and metatags for photos so that they appear in "image searches" for the given keyword.

- The most important metatag is the page title. It appears above the toolbar of the browser.

- An effective page title metatag contains one to three keywords. Depending on the context of the content, you may include your brand name.

- Both web and mobile browsers tend to truncate title displays. That's why it's best to start your title tag with a keyword.

- The most optimal title tags have less than 70 characters and are no longer than ten words. Anything longer than that would make

☐   bots shy away from your content.

☐   Descriptive meta titles work well for social sharing. This is why you must prioritize clickable and eye-catching title tags.

-What's with Meta Descriptions

The meta description is the page description metatag. Like the meta title, it also appears on SERP. It is the page description below the title tag. An appealing and comprehensive description that can immediately offer an answer to the search query (keywords) can bolster the rank of a page.

Bing and Google truncate meta descriptions to 120 characters. Like tweets, page descriptions have limited characters. If your page doesn't have a meta description, search engines will display the first sentences in your introduction.

How about the meta description and meta tags for social media pages? The purpose of social meta tags is to manipulate the way your digital content is displayed in users' home pages and news feeds, instead of letting the social platforms generate the image, description, and headline of your post.

By optimizing your social meta tags, you can control the presentation of your posts and tweets. In your social network, you can also drive outside sources towards the right audience.

When sharing URLs of articles, especially those with images or videos, you need to make your post appealing, so that it could entice people, increase web traffic, and generate leads. It would be best if it contains the following elements:

✓   Link

✓   Enticing description

✓   Correct name

✓ High-definition images

Twitter, Facebook, Instagram, and other social networks get the parameters from your blog or website. By using social media meta tags, you can control what they pull from your source, which could be your blog or YouTube video. For example, you can use open graph tags. You just have to embed it in the HTML code of your published post.

If you use open graph meta tags in your WordPress blog article and shared its link on Instagram, you can control what will appear on your Instagram timeline. This works the same way on Twitter.

Nowadays, most websites encourage and entice visitors to share their pages on social channels, specifically Twitter and Facebook. In the eyes of entertained prospects, the sharing buttons are begging to be clicked.

Search Engine Optimization for Your Website and social media

SEO is the process of making edits to your blog, website, or social media profiles in order to rank high on SERP. If you implement search engine optimization properly, search engines will discover your posts and profile with their spider bots.

Now, how can that happen?

-Writing your first optimized paragraph

You now know how to manipulate the appearance of your content on search engines and social media. You've also learned how to incorporate keywords in your meta titles and headlines.

So, it's time to write the introduction of your first search engine-friendly digital content. This could be a blog, product review, video description, or social media post.

Nevertheless, it needs to be optimized. The meta title and page description could be the first thing that bots scan in your digital content. This is why you need keywords visible in the title of the content and at the beginning of the page's text.

In addition to that, insert at least one to two keywords in your introduction, but avoid stuffing them with each other. SEO experts, like Neil Patel and Vanessa Fox, say that keyword density should be around 1% to 2%. This implies that a keyword or keyword phrase should appear 1 to 2 times per 100 words.

Most bloggers and social media marketers only use one keyword or keyword phrase per 100 words, to avoid keyword stuffing. You may use at least two, but make sure they're somewhat apart from each other.

Google's example of keyword stuffing:

> We sell *custom cigar humidors*. Our *custom cigar humidors* are handmade. If you're thinking of buying a *custom cigar humidor*, please contact our *custom cigar humidor* specialists at *custom.cigar.humidor*@example.com.

In the image above, the italicized words are the keywords. Too many search terms are used in a short paragraph. That is an example of keyword stuffing.

-Update Often to Please the Web Arachnids

Search engines, particularly Google, prefer updated content. The same goes for Instagram, Twitter, and Tiktok. Google bots index updated articles, as well as the most recent social media posts higher than old content.

Once or twice a month, change a paragraph or insert fresh content in your top or most valuable web pages. You must include this in your content publishing schedule. If you can't commit to such a task, ask your content manager or web developer to do it for you. You may also set automatic publishing or schedule posts.

For social media marketing, you can use free tools, like Twitter's pending post tool and FB's post scheduling.

-Tags and Images

Have you ever thought of using keywords in the images you post online? Will that even do any good for your SMM strategy? It will and bear astounding results.

Of course, you'll only use high-quality and royalty-free images in your blog and social media posts. But beautiful and appealing images are invisible in the digital world if no one can see them.

In other words, they're useless if you leave them as they are. And the effort you've put into editing and looking for that perfect image for your content is null—insignificant.

That's why you need SEO, whether for your text content or digital media, such as images and videos. If you've effectively optimized the text of your web content, then your visuals will be seen, and many will appreciate it.

If you combine text optimization, image <alt> tags, and timely updates, you can increase the probability that your post will end up on SERP's first page. Even if it doesn't, its visuals may appear on Google or Bing's "image searches."

Now, here's the million-dollar question. "How to optimize an image for search engines and social media platforms?" All you need to do is insert one to four keywords in the filename, caption, <alt> tags, and nearby text. This is actually easier than article optimization.

-What Matters to Search Engines

When it comes to disliking things, web crawlers are like humans. They dislike things that are low-quality, unorganized, and improperly labeled. You will hate it if you use bleach powder, instead of flour, when cooking your favorite snack bars, just because your spouse mislabeled the containers.

Spiderbots behave the same way. They will rank your site favorably if you avoid things that they don't like.

Computers are getting smarter. However, even artificial intelligence-powered programs like web crawlers still can't read the context of images posted online.

Marketers, like you, must feed them with relevant keywords so that they can scan the valuable information and relevant messages in your multimedia. And you need to avoid some things they flag as undesirable content. If you implement any of the following practices, search engines will penalize you.

- ☐ Low-quality graphics and images without description

Photographers and artists prefer web pages without words but search engine bots hate them. When optimizing, avoid these two. In the previous section, it's detailed how to leverage high-quality images.

- ☐ Flash visuals

Whether your developer is telling you to include flash animation, or you want to add them because they seem cool and enthralling, GIFs and Flash animations can also affect site speed.

Spiderbots prefer fast loading times, and users coming from regions with poor connectivity will face a hard time seeing your content. If there are better options, they will head there. This means if your website loads poorly due to flash visuals, your prospects may go to other sites.

Plus, some search engines can't index Flash content. Mobile phone browsers and Computers with MAC OS also detests flash. Google bots can read flash. But. since it affects loading times, the bots ofen give web pages with GIFs or flash images a lower rank than those that have none. It's better to include a video than a flash visual. Videos have clearer previews than flash files too.

☐ Duplicate content

This is another reason why plagiarism is a big no-no. At all times, you must provide original and unique content. Even the use of identical sub-headings will make the crawlers flag your post.

Also, even if you've archived the content, search engines will still index the hidden page and the contents in it. So, if you deleted a blog post and it still sits in the online archives, the crawlers will flag your recycled content.

Copywriters avoid this. For example, they may have posted a promotional post on Facebook and eventually deleted it. That post is still in their trash. Although other FB users can't see it anymore, the crawlers still can.

Gaining Traction on Search Engines with Your Social Channels

The boom of many social media platforms forced many search engines to adjust their algorithms. There are many different SNS websites out there, and they handle social media searches differently. For example, Yahoo and Google also index and ranks social media pages and published posts that contain relevant keywords.

However, they don't include private posts. Additionally, you may need to consider using search websites, like SocialSearch, so that you can check real-time results for IG, Twitter, and YouTube.

Bing generates its SERPs differently. In regular search results, Bing displays topical posts from internet icons, public figures, and influencers. These are served even without surfers needing to log in to their social media accounts.

But some sections in SNS platforms are only accessible by logging in. Another way to increase your reach is to use Pinterest and its functions. In fact, you can pin your hopes to the platform. Google spider now crawls pins, boards, and hashtags on Pinterest. The bots look for relevant descriptions and keywords

-Monitor Your Search Engine Ranking

Reports on search engine rankings are integral to the success of your brand. Such data can help you identify performance trends and determine the level of your online reach. There are free-to-use programs that aid in reading the reports. By knowing more about your performance online, you can further improve your marketing plan and advertising campaigns.

For example, SEMrush offers a metric that measures "visibility." It's quite different from your run-of-the-mill rankers and metric counters.

When you're engaging in social media marketing, you need to monitor your brand's performance. You must know the position of your brand in the industry. How can you do that? This is when the free online tools in the list below can come in handy.

- ✓ ZoomRank
- ✓ SERank
- ✓ Search Engine Rankings
- ✓ Rank Tracker
- ✓ Moz Rank Checker
- ✓ CheckMoz

Social media profiles and posts appear on search engines by page or keyword. Most ranking programs charge users, but some offer their services free of charge. Although they only rank a limited number of keywords or pages, you can use these ranking services for free. If you have a tight budget, opt for this option.

-SEO and SMM

Overall, search engine optimization is for improving the quality and quantity of web traffic to your website or social media page. Attaining a high ranking when a surfer searches for a keyword related to your topic can increase the visibility of your brand online. This provides more opportunities for increasing profit and generating leads.

Both SEO and SMM are long-term strategies. After you optimize and post something, you don't just leave it there. Even if it does gain instant traction, you need to regularly work on it. Updates, engagements, and responses are necessary, and they strengthen the foundation of the two marketing practices.

You can implement SMM without SEO. However, you'll achieve better results by combining the two. Understanding both SMM and SEO can help you perform better on social channels and search engine results.

Research for SEO, brand voice, and social media persona can help you know the needs and wants of your prospects. The bottom line is SMM and SEO aids each other and they bear astounding results when combined.

How Do Social Media Algorithms Work?

For the average person, social media plays a massive role in his/her life. How about you? How many hours per day do you spend on social media, which includes YouTube and Pinterest?

In 2017, Facebook was the 3rd most visited site on the web, next to Google and YouTube. With millions of users browsing on such websites, the order needs to be created and search results must provide relevant results. Algorithms and spider bots do just that.

Depending on the social media platform you're using, the search results and how posts are generated on your home page will differ. Algorithms dictate what your followers see and how many people can actually see your post.

As a marketer, you've two options. You can either let the algorithms do their work or play with them to your advantage.

-What Exactly are Social Media Algorithms?

Basically, algorithms are mathematical sets of rules. They specify how data groups behave. On social media, they maintain order and aids in providing accurate and systemic ranking results.

In 2020, there were 4 billion unique internet users. Among them, approximately 3 billion were active on social media. That's about 43% of the world's population. That's a myriad of people to manage and monitor.

Enter algorithms--series of instructions—sets of rules—that tells networks, programs, and computers how to operate, read data, and provide results. In essence, algorithms are instructions followed by artificial intelligence-powered programs that solve problems and execute inputted commands.

-The Different Types of Social Media Algorithms

On every online platform, algorithms vary. The algorithms on Facebook and Instagram are different, despite being sister companies. In this section, you'll be acquainted with the number one social media algorithm cheat sheet on the web.

☐ Facebook

Customer engagement is the primary key to this social media giant's algorithm layout. They're designed to greatly intensify the viewership and importance of friendly, familial, and local posts.

In generating results, Facebook prefers relationships and friendly connections over business posts. Nevertheless, there are ways to get around the restrictions that the algorithms have imposed.

Facebook ranks paid contents separately. Still, the ranking of promoted ads also revolves around relevance, engagement, and customer response. User-friendliness is the primary key. The other keys are listed below. These are some of the industry's secrets.

- ✓ Facebook users often see the post of pages and profiles that they often engage with. If they often like a post of a specific page or profile, then the most recent published content from that account will appear on the user's news feed.

- ✓ Posts with many lengthy comments and high engagement will likely show up in the news feeds of the people that always interact with the page.

- ✓ Posts with many varied reactions, such as hearts, likes, and care emojis are also prioritized by Facebook.

- ✓ The most recent posts from your top friends and the people or pages you engage with from time to time will likely appear on your home feed.

Here are some more tips for taking advantage Facebook algorithms:

- ✓ Post when your friends and likers are active. You must consider and think about the people you need to reach. Are they on Facebook? What time do they use the platform?

- ✓ Use high-quality videos. According to SproutSocial, videos are the most viewed content on Facebook. Many users will watch your videos if you showcase an interesting thumbnail.

- ✓ Use polls and giveaways to drive your engagement and impressions up. In a positive way, bait your audience to post reactions and comments. However, avoid asking likes, shares, and comments in each of your posts. If you do so, Facebook will start to label your published content as "spam."

- ✓ Ask, request, or encourage your close contacts, including your relatives, friends, and colleagues, to share your posts to their groups and other channels on the platform. This can greatly amplify the reach and impressions of your posts.

- ✓ Prioritize photos and tags over external links. Inserting external links, like URLs from your blog or website, is fine. But it needs to be optimized. You can learn how to do that in the following sections. If you optimize your content, you can increase the traffic on your website with Facebook.

- ✓ Facebook, unlike other social media platforms, such as Twitter and Twitch, prefers to keep users and content on their own website. Constant linking of external sources can negatively affect your rank in news feeds.

☐ Instagram

Instagram is Facebook's sister company, so you can expect that there are some similarities with the algorithms of the two platforms. Despite this, Instagram's algorithms are trickier to master than Facebook's. Nevertheless, a cheat list has been prepared just for marketers like you.

- ✓ The platform prioritizes posts with many likes. A post with a thousand likes will generate more engagements and impressions than those with just tens or hundreds of reactions.

- ✓ The most recent posts of profiles with high engagement rates are also rank high on feeds. Posts by profiles that a given user always engages with are often presented to that user's home page on the platform.

✓   Posts with hashtags that many people follow are also rank higher than those with irrelevant tags.

✓   Occasionally, Instagram will generate posts from a profile with high engagement that the user doesn't follow.

✓   To encourage comments and likes, ask questions in the captions. You can ask your audience to share their similar experiences in the comment sections.

✓ If you already have a strong following, wherein many people are admiring you and are always waiting for your next post, then ask them to send likes. Promise them that when a post of yours will have attained a specific number of likes or comments, you'll reveal something about yourself.

✓   Instagram's algorithms for hashtag application change from time to time, so it's best to experiment every time. For best results, you need to have a dummy account where you can check for the changes and test the reception of a specific tag.

✓ If IG has something that Twitter offers is its 100% organic reach with IG Stories. This feature can drive your brand's offers in front of your online follower's news feeds. However, you'll only see its effects if you have many followers.

✓   Be consistent. On every social media platform, consistency is a must. Rebranding or changing the context of your contents will not only affect the view of your followers about your page, but it will also make the algorithm downgrade your recent and future posts. This will happen if you consecutively provide something different from your usual posts.

✓ Engage with your followers and brands similar to yours. Staying active daily on Instagram is as important as regularly posting enthralling content. This is also true for Twitter. In fact, you can stay relevant on Twitter by just sending likes and retweeting content that is relevant to your niche.

☐ Twitter

Among other social media platforms, Twitter is considered unique. This social platform generates tweets by relation to the user and by date and time posted. Twitter may seem the lowest ranked in today's top social networks, but user-friendly and marketing-friendly features and functions will surely not disappoint you.

✓ Fresh material ranks higher than day-old tweets.

✓ The number of engagements a post has greatly influences its ranking.

✓ Users will typically use tweets from profiles and pages they often or have recently interacted with. Tweets with high engagement, like comments and retweets, related to their interest will also generate in their news feed.

✓ For best results, tweet daily so that you'll stay relevant to your followers.

✓ When sharing something relevant or informative, use all 280 characters.

✓ Branded or otherwise, hashtags allow you to gain good traction on Twitter.

✓ Tweets with GIFs, videos, and photos get more impressions and reactions.

✓ With moving graphics, you can request feedback or answer a question you've included in your tweet.

- ✓ Join Twitter chats and relevant topics and trends. Be part of conversations in your industry. This can increase the odds of your tweet appearing on many feeds.

- ✓ Respond to comments every 2 to 3 hours. This makes your post reappear again on home pages. Also, you must reserve at least 1 to 3 comments to reply to. In doing so, you can make your tweet appear on news feeds again, making the tweet recent even after days of posting.

The algorithms on other social media platforms are discussed in their respective chapters. In recent years, social media platforms have prioritized user-friendly content. Some platforms, like Twitter and Pinterest, give tweets with hashtags a higher rank than others. This is because hashtags encourage users to publish relevant, engaging, and high-quality content.

What's Passive Income?

Basically, passive income is your earnings from ways that require little to no daily effort. With a stable source of passive income, you can earn while you sleep. Examples of passive income include the profits you get from stock investments and your commissions in affiliate sales. Your payment for Youtube ads and ad revenues are also forms of passive income.

You can use social media to earn passive income directly or you can use it to buff up your current passive income streams, such as the revenue get from guest posting, blogging, and product commissions.

-Why Set-up Passive Income Streams

Establishing one or more sources of income is a great way to secure your future and diversify your financial portfolio.

On top of all that, you can focus on "living" your life. A passive income stream may seem daunting to establish, but they'll allow you to breathe more easily in the coming years.

Once you're acquired a lot of money from your many endeavors, you can just sit back and relax. You'll have the time to read books and catch up with the paperbacks you've bought but have never read. You can also spend your free time upgrading your existing skills and gaining new ones. As you expand your knowledge, you can also earn in other fields.

With a diverse financial portfolio, you can establish your life, family, and future faster than your peers. You can finally say that you're really living your life. You can also focus on your family, your hobbies, and the other things you love.

Your source of money, whether it is corporate job or your your business endeavors, is your wealth-building tool. Even if you're currently in love with your job, you'll definitely say no to another income stream that requires minimal effort. You won't mind earning extra cash that doesn't require many tears, time, and blood. Here are more benefits that passive income streams can bring to your life:

- ✓ Improve your plans and allow you to achieve them faster than normal
- ✓ Allow you to retire early, probably at 30, 35, or 40
- ✓ Protect you from complete loss and allow you to avoid abject poverty in case of a depression or a nationwide economical collapse
- ✓ Provide extra cash sources for yourself and the things you love.

Personal Brand vs. Small Business

Branding is an integral part of your online success. Your brand, whether personal or professional, need to be consistent. It's the representation of your skills and experiences that you have accumulated over the years. It also serves as the emblem of your core values and the goals that drive your online endeavors forward.

With your brand, you'll build relationships with others on the web. Such connections will serve as the vital foundation to your advertising campaigns and marketing plans. Now, it's up to you to choose whether you'll opt for a personal brand or a small business that has a corporate appeal.

The former offers more freedom in the virtual world; the latter allows you to grow in a more professional setting. If you desire to hire freelancers to launch a startup, then you should go for a business brand and proceed to establish a small business.

This section will let you delve into the differences that exist between the two, as well as their pros and cons. At the comfort of your own home, you can choose to become a CEO or a freelancer. With just your social media and personal computer, you can even achieve both.

-What Exactly is a Personal Brand?

Your personal brand is built around you, your skills, and your personality. It could also be based on your interests and lifestyle. Similar to a business brand, your personal brand can be further defined and clearly represented by your logo, tagline, web bio, and social media.

Personal branding lets you position yourself and your services as a credible and trustworthy entity in your industry. Between social media accounts and personal websites, it can be easy to formulate a personal brand than a professional brand. Here are some more advantages of opting for a personal brand:

☐ Flexibility

With a personal brand, you can use your name or even the name of your pet. But you still need to make the name easy to remember. And it must be relevant to your industry.

Also, personal brands are easy to rebrand. If you begin to offer something different, you can easily adapt and modify your marketing plans, without having to change important things. You don't have to create a new social media account, wherein you'll have to start from scratch again.

Personal brands are great for streamers, vloggers, podcasters, and anyone wishing to have a speaking career online. Once you've nurtured a fan base and you've many followers, you will start to be seen as someone reliable. Having this kind of image is very important in any niche or industry.

For a one-person industry, a personal brand can be easier to handle than a professional brand

In case you're an author, coach, artist, or professional speaker, having a strong personal brand can boost your exposure and attract interested prospects. In the said fields, prospects prefer friendly icons that are easy to talk to and that exudes their real personality.

Plus, it pays to be unique in those niches. However, if you're representing an entity or organization, that's a different matter.

-Knowing more about Small Business Brands

This is your alternative to a personal brand. Small business brands are centered around the identity you've created for your business. Most times, the title of your small business must be independent from your personal goals. Instead, your business goals should serve as its foundations.

Like a personal brand, it has pros and cons. These are covered below. Nevertheless, with a business brand, you can brand anything, from yourself to your ideas.

Indeed, business brands can take more upfront work. But you can also think of it as an extension of your personal brand. Branding isn't only about creating a name, but you must consider a lot of things like tone, voice, and target audience. These are all discussed in the following chapters. It must also represent the values you stand for, as well as the services you plan to provide.

While branding your small business and developing an identity online, you must highlight your strengths and the resources that can help you serve your client base. You need a brand--an identity—that your prospective customers can connect with and that can meet their needs.

Hence, a business brand must be based on the behaviors, needs, and interests of your prospects. It also needs authentic goals and prime values centered on your industry.

For example, if you're offering painting services and you prefer a business brand, then you must prioritize the deadlines set by your clients. You must prioritize it over your own schedule. Why go as far as this? Your client will give you a partial payment for your freelance service. Since you've accepted a form of payment, you, the freelancer, must uphold his requirements and the fulfillment of the service the client has requested.

Successful business branding should be an ongoing process. It requires audience data and analytics results to craft messages that can resonate with online users needing your services.

Should you take the long walk and choose a business brand? Or will you settle for a more personal branding process? Sit down, contemplate, and consider your resources, and as the last step, consider the pros and cons of the two types of branding for small businesses.

-The Pros

- A business brand could be better for you if you're planning for long-term growth plans

Some freelancers will not settle with just being a freelancer till their retirement. Some desire to upgrade their career potentials and to take more steps ahead from where they presently are.

- You can position yourself and your business in the virtual world's front stalls

There, web traffic is rife. These positions are the equivalent of the front stalls in the physical world. Complement your brand with a professional and eye-catching tagline. With this, you'll be heading towards a successful start. You'll see that your ideal clients can easily grasp what you offer. If you combine these two with a comprehensive bio, then your prospects will avoid having to ask basic questions about your brand.

- Business brands are remarkably easy to sell

In particular industries, like advertising, data mining, digital marketing, and human resources, clients prefer a professional brand over a personal one. Hence, you can attract more clients and land more deals because the said industries are the most active right now in the online world. If you aim to have a small agency, then you must definitely choose a professional brand.

- You can attract investors

Investors prefer business brands. Also, when franchising or selling a brand name, the buyers favor that that is not named after the creator. A developed and recognizable brand is what clients are willing to pay for.

-Small Business Brand Cons

- It's harder to build a business brand

A business brand takes time to build. In branding or rebranding, you may opt to hire an experienced digital marketer or do the work yourself. Either of the two isn't an instant process.

It can take weeks or even months before you can officially launch a business with a solid branding. You may need a professional-looking website, optimized content (e.g., bios, taglines, and profile intros), high-quality headers, or other types of graphics for your online profiles.

The requirement to have a website will depend upon your budget. Today, social media platforms already provide the functions that websites with a registered domain offer.

For example, eCommerce businesses can benefit from Instagram's collaboration with Shopify. This ultra new feature allows anyone, even those who have no IG business account, to set up a shopping section on the said platform. This can work well for those who prefer personal brands.

With a business brand, you definitely need a proper website. Many high-quality visuals and graphics are also required.

☐ Professional brands aren't flexible

In case your interest changes or you want to jump to another industry, you may not be able to reuse your brand and the social profiles you've built around it. This means you can lose your following and avid followers. You've to start from scratch, again.

Yes, you can craft another name for your new services or products, and you can modify your tagline. However, when changing fields, your old brand, which was based on different ideals and services, may not work for the new one.

Identifying Your Goals and Your Target Audience

Without goals, it can be hard to formulate a marketing plan. Monitoring the results of a campaign will also be a challenge. Clear goals can propel your strategy forward. In measuring results, your objectives aid in defining priorities and metrics.

To help you get a head start, here are some examples of social media marketing goals:

- ✓ Generate traffic to your website.
- ✓ Advertise a service
- ✓ Sell a product
- ✓ Form connections and build rapport with prospects
- ✓ Communicate with clients or buyers
- ✓ Establish authority online
- ✓ Launch an exposure campaign

-Beginning with a Broad Objective

Firstly, ask yourself, "Why am I putting my business on social media?" There are many forms of digital marketing, including internet marketing, PPC campaigns, and social media marketing.

The answer to that question could serve as your very first goal. As a startup, you must get your brand and your services to the right audience in the virtual world. Yes, there's a myriad of people on social channels every day. However, you'll get nowhere if you serve your content to the wrong group.

In crafting your first objectives, you need to visualize your wants and aims. You may use a word document to list them all down. For reference, here are some examples:

- ✓ For an enterprise company, some of your goals could be "providing timely customer service" and "boosting customer loyalty."

✓ Startups and those with personal brands can start with improving brand awareness and reach.

✓ Small businesses, once done with branding, should proceed to improving engagement and increasing lead generation rate.

By listing down your objectives for your brand, you can start thinking about granular, specific goals. In turn, they can inspire your daily social activities. Remember, you may just waste your time on social media if you don't have clear goals in mind. You'll be going around in circles.

-Setting SMART Marketing Goals

To realize your goal, it must have the following characteristics: smart, measurable, attainable, and realistic. This is the formula for setting SMART goals. In the digital marketing world, SMART goals are a prominent goal-setting framework.

Now, take a closer look at what makes this strategy smart:

☐ Specific

The more specific your goal is, the easier it is for you to see the things you need to achieve. "Growing Twitter followers" and "expanding brand reach" are some examples of specific goals.

Their opposites are "improving lead generation" and "increasing engagement." Both of these marketing strategies involve many elements, and also, they could mean many things.

For example, lead generation could imply that you want to increase your sales, or you desire to turn viewers into subscribers.

☐ Measurable

Without an exact or an approximate figure, your marketing efforts could be all over the place. For your brand, what do you want to achieve in social media? Do you want a thousand followers every week? Do you aim to have 100,000 followers in just one month?

Once you have that in mind, you must ask yourself, "Is that figure attainable within the time frame I've set?" If you're just new to Twitter and you aim to garner 100,000 followers in one month, you may not achieve that goal.

Unless you plan to employ services that give Twitter accounts 100,000 spam, untargeted, and irrelevant follows.

- [ ] Attainable

Twitter has restrictions when it comes to the number of activities you can do every day, and so do Facebook, Instagram, Tiktok, and YouTube. This means there's a limit to how many "likes" and "follows" you can do on the platform every day.

Can you attain your set goals? Can you double the number of your followers in a week? In this phase, considering the factors that affect your objectives and goals is definitely a must!

For example, by yourself, you can't generate 500 mutual followings in one day because Twitter restricts every account to only 400 follows per day. Going over that limit will have your account suspended. If you ignore Twitter's warnings, you may not be able to access your social media profile forever.

- [ ] Relevant

The content you serve and all the elements in your social media profile should be aligned with your objectives. That's why your goals need to be aligned with your business' visions and values. Also, every activity you make on social channels must bring value to your customers/followers.

- [ ] Time-specific

Goals need deadlines. Set a specific time frame at which you can virtually achieve your targets with the skills and resources you have. For large goals, try subdividing them into mini feats that you can accomplish in shorter periods.

Setting SMART goals guarantees social media marketing success. According to SAMSHA and SmartMarketing, SMART goals stabilize businesses and make long-term success possible. Once you have a broad objective in mind, you can proceed to define your goals that are specific, measurable, attainable, relevant, and time specific. Once done with this phase, you can track metrics or key performance indicators (KPIs).

For accurate results, use free social analytics tools, including the built-in tools on social media platforms, such as FB Analytics and Twitter Analytics.

Lastly, you must visit your goals regularly and check daily reports. Always remind yourself the goals you need to achieve and the values that your business must adhere to.

By doing so, you can determine whether you're on the right track or something requires adjustment. Remember, a winning formula needs measurement, modification, and proper execution.

-Defining Your Social Media Target Audience

For marketers, their target audience is their client base. For internet icons, they need likers, viewers, followers, or subscribers. Their leads could be anyone who can meet their set goals, which could be getting likes, garnering a specific number of views, or landing freelancing projects.

Below is the step-by-step process for finding the right target audience on any social media platform.

1) Set your business goals.
2) Create a brand voice.

3) Create or identify buyer personas.

4) Know which social channels are your personas most active in.

5) Study your competitors and the people who interact with them online.

6) Know the top search terms, keywords, and hashtags they use. This can come in handy when you're marketing on Instagram, Pinterest, and Twitter. YouTube also makes use of "tags" and "keywords."

7) Survey potential clients and scout hashtags, groups, forums, and other online communities they may be using.

Defining your target audience is quite similar to creating a buyer persona, but it involves a couple more steps. Nevertheless, both can help you create proper brand guidelines.

You can also finally find the answers to questions like the following:

✓ What digital content will your audience relate to?

✓ What voice or tone will allow you to connect more with your prospects?

With your target audience defined, you can easily establish rapport with your prospects, prompt them to interact with you, and fulfill your other SMART goals.

Your target audience, or the people who will interact with your brand, make purchases, or fulfill other goals, must be properly defined and detailed. By doing so, you won't leave any individual who might be interested in your offers.

Outline of the Book

With "Mastering Social Media Algorithms," you'll learn the best forms of SMM in a step-by-step way.

If you're still new to social media marketing, then chapter 1 can introduce you to the world of SMM. It contains a wealth of information that every budding marketer should know.

From keyword research to platform algorithms, chapter 1 "The Essential Guide to Social Media Marketing" will serve as your steppingstone to easily learn every lesson in this book.

Chapter 2 "Growing Your Brand and Your Business with Great Content" is the bridge to all of the other chapters. There are two prerequisites to any form of SMM, including Twitch advertising and YouTube marketing.

The first one is high-quality content. This could be text-based posts, audio clips, or recorded videos. As a marketer and brand manager, and digital media or web content you publish on social channels must be of high quality.

Providing low-resolution images or publishing videos with bad audio can be detrimental to the business you're handling. This could stain the brand's image and make you lose prospective customers.

The second one is having a decent number of loyal followers. As much as you need relevant information, you need a targeted audience. They must be able to appreciate the things you offer on your social media.

Prospects are the people who you can turn into leads. Leads are meant to fulfill specific actions or goals. This includes sharing a comment, retweeting an image, making a purchase, and many more. All of these are further discussed in chapter 2.

Once you know the ups and downs of creating engaging and enticing content, you can proceed to the rest of the chapters. In this book, Twitter is the first social media to be introduced.

Chapter 3 "Marketing on Twitter" provides real-life examples of social media marketing. In this chapter, you'll know more about Twitter algorithms and how to use the functions of the platform to your advantage.

When you reach chapter 4, you'll be introduced to YouTube marketing. You can also finally gain the skill of creating viral videos, trending on the "suggested page," and increasing your subscribers by the thousands.

Chapter 5 provides everything you need to know about IG marketing, including bonus sections for making your IG profile into an eCommerce shop. Here, you'll learn how to properly set up an Instagram business account, the things to avoid on the platform, and developing and launching ads on the channel.

Chapter 6 and 7 introduce you to two budding social platforms that originally started as video-sharing sites. The statistics show that Twitch and TikTok could be the next YouTube. And you can learn how to become an internet icon on the said platforms.

At the end of your journey to improving your business through social media, the very last part of this book can help you continue on the right path. The same can be said with the many snippets of knowledge in "Mastering Social Media Algorithms."

CHAPTER 2: GROWING YOUR BRAND AND YOUR BUSINESS WITH GREAT CONTENT

Thanks to the World Wide Web, today is a good time to establish a business. With just your skills and an internet connection, you can launch your very own brand. Once it grows, you can register it as a valid business entity in order to improve your credibility.

Online, you've the ability to employ a variety of tools and services to grow your business. Most of them are free. The top social media platforms, including Instagram and YouTube, as well as the free services they offer, are some example marketing tools.

Creating high-quality and delectable content and using such tools allow you to promote your business or personal brand for both local and global audiences.

Digital Marketing at a Glance

If you're planning to dab in social media to grow your name online, you've probably heard the term "content marketing." Content marketing is basically the process or practice of utilizing images, videos, podcasts, and blog posts to promote a service or product. It's a type of digital marketing which is primarily used in SEO and SMM.

Content marketing includes keyword research and search engine optimization. It involves techniques that can boost the marketability of a brand, product, or service. In SMM, content marketing should be employed when creating advertisement campaigns and when scheduling and optimizing future posts.

For example, you offer "organic" foodstuffs, and you want people to find your business online. You specifically desire that Vegans see your products and "how good you've grown them." For this to happen, you need to publish content that your prospects, which include vegans and other health enthusiasts, can actually see and appreciate. If you offer fresh fruits and vegetables and you use grainy and low-quality images, your desire won't come true.

Firstly, you must of the type of people who visit farmer's markets. Ask yourself, "what kind of content will attract them? Do you plan to cater to Gen Zs, Millennials, or Boomers? Each group of people has specific standard preferences. Colorful banners and images may attract Gen Z's, but that could make Boomers turn around and look for another option. Now, where can you use internet marketing to solve such a dilemma?

For example, it's apple season and many are evidently looking for local organic shops that can provide fresh, sweet, and juicy apples. To attract such people, you can create articles or short social media posts that can make leads redirect to your website. What should the content contain? Valuable information is required. The text and the digital media inserted into it should also be of high quality and has a spice of persuasion and self-promotion that isn't too obvious.

When readers finally land on your website or online shop, content marketing can do its magic. They'll see the links to your other pages and content, as wells as anchor texts that can help them contact you. To get the best out of every situation, you should also provide information about upcoming sales, your other products, and special events.

Content marketing aims to drive people to a specific location and achieve marketing goals. Often, digital marketers use SMM and content marketing hand in hand.

What will you learn from this chapter?

✓ Develop social media content that can stand out from rival brands

✓ Use digital content to sell and promote your brand online

✓ Consider the best social media platform for your brand/business

✓ Be acquainted with everything you need to know about content marketing

Everything you can see online is considered digital content—even the logo of your business rival could be a part of a content marketing strategy. The following elements are also used in this type of digital marketing.

✓ Charts
✓ Infographics
✓ Video
✓ Radio
✓ Moving images
✓ Podcasts
✓ Written word
✓ Images
✓ Website backgrounds

Digital content can teach or amuse, but it's also a powerful marketing tool for enticing searchers and search engines. Many entities are seeing positive results by incorporating various content. They're able to raise brand awareness and reach the right people.

Those are the users who could be interested in what you do. Do you offer freelance services? Then, you need clients who are seeking a service that you can offer. Do you run an eCommerce shop? Then, you need to entice prospects that need your products. This chapter will not only introduce content marketing to you but will also teach you how to use great content for social media marketing.

Making Your Social Media Posts Standout

All of your marketing and content creation efforts will be for naught if only a few people can see it. If you can't even compel the people closest to you to share your content, then you'll have a hard time getting impressions. One impression is equal to one moment your post gets displayed on a user's home page.

For example, follower X liked your video content on Twitter. All of his online followers, who are into your niche, will also see your post if they head to their home page on the same day of posting or a day or two after that. The time frame depends on the number of "followings" they have.

To have the kind of content that people view or read on social media, you need to take steps and learn strategies that can make your posts stand out. Despite what you see on YouTube and Facebook, there are many ways to make viral content other than using the faces of cute cats.

Are you wondering about these industry secrets? Just continue reading to learn more about them.

☐ Show Purpose

Remember, don't post content for the sake of posting. If you make something hasty just for "showing something," the content may not even be in line with your page's purpose. It's always best to *schedule your posts*.

Too much and too little posting can decrease engagements and page views. In particular, most Twitter and Instagram users click the Unfollow button when their home pages are spammed by the activity of particular users. Likewise, they stop following pages that have no "recent activities." This remains true on the top five social media platforms.

Again, don't post content for the sake of posting. Otherwise, your content will seem bland, forced, confusing, or redundant.

- ☐ Provide Value

The rule of thumb is to provide valuable content that readers or viewers can use, appreciate, and relate to. By providing value, you encourage sharing and interaction.

Blog and social media content should be much more than just publishing bland captions or copy-pasted text. Whenever you're publishing anything online, do consider the following tips so that your efforts will not go in vain:

- ✓ If your digital media, like a video or meme image, makes people laugh, then it's valuable! If a blog or social media post teaches something and is unbiased and non-pretentious, then it has value and people will view it positively.
- ✓ If a tweet is like a breaking news, then it's also valuable.
- ✓ If your IG image provides info or motivation, then it has value.

In addition, you've to personalize your posts and contents. It must carry your brand gracefully and succinctly--in a brief and clearly expressed manner.

- ☐ Answer an Inquiry

If users are searching for a specific piece of information and land on your page/social media, ask yourself, "Will they read the whole content?" "Will they click on the link?" Your post should answer the question "Why am I here?"

☐ Be Unique

As much as possible, you must be unique. Avoid copying the quirks, styles, and contents of other people in your niche. By doing this, you're inviting haters and making people lose respect for you.

If you've no originality, your followers will get tired of your content. If one time an avid follower of yours notice that you're just presenting an imitation, then you may lose him/her forever.

☐ Be Relatable

People on social media like to watch videos and read stories and blogs. If they like the content or they can relate to it, they'll nod in agreement. For instance, a funny cat video that shows a kitten meowing pitifully while being bathed will prompt dedicated cat owners to laugh and share the video. This is because they've likely laughed at the same situation! That's why it's important to study your niche and consider the preferences of your prospects.

☐ Utilize keywords

Proper use of keywords can boost organic traffic. The phrase "organic marketing" refers to any strategy that generates traffic to businesses without using any form of paid advertisement. Any form of brand promotion or content marketing that requires zero dime, like Facebook updates, unpaid tweets, guest posts, case studies, and blog posts, are all under organic marketing.

According to Marilyn Wilkinson, a copywriter and digital marketer at Full Stack Copywriter, organic visibility on the major search engines in the world is integral for reaching set internet marketing goals and for boosting brand awareness KPI. Marilyn says, "Otherwise, you're leaving the door open for your rivals to steal customers and prospects right under your nose. Neil Patel, Dan Lok, and Marilyn

Wilkinson all use keyword optimization in their marketing and copywriting endeavors.

Using keywords in the introduction and in some subheadings is just one effective practice. But there's more to it than just that. Professional marketers employ many techniques and strategies.

For one, targeting organic keywords via search engine optimization can keep you on the radar of your prospects. Those who will use the words and phrases included in your content when searching for services that you offer might see your headline and article!

Another option aside from organic traffic is "integration with other marketing channels, like social media platforms and video-sharing websites." If you indeed use money in such platforms, do so for paid campaigns. However, only do this if you have a solid marketing strategy and effective search engine optimization plan.

Take social media platforms as an example. The combination of search engine optimization with social media marketing is a match made in heaven. Together, they can help create rapport, connect with your target audience, and improve brand exposure. What's more, content on social channels gets indexed by crawlers as well. This includes descriptions in YouTube videos and tweets with hashtags.

☐ Use Appealing Visuals

A vibrant, colorful, and intriguing photo can enthrall readers and make them crave for more. This can boost engagement! It can also make your post more relatable. High-quality digital media incorporated in an engaging and relatable story can generate many likes, comments, and shares.

In fact, online content can experience an approximately 40% rise in engagement if compelling visual content is inserted. Additionally, content with a high-quality digital media can go viral and help prospects and audiences to better appreciate or understand the purpose of the post. It can subconsciously convey your brand message, which could be the main purpose of your marketing endeavors.

For instance, your message will be better received if you back it with a relevant high-quality nature photo. Also, you need to make a part of your post clickable. If it goes viral, it could bring in inbound links and generate high traffic.

Make sure that your brand logo is included in the post. With inbound links and hashtags, your content will be more relevant, It can up to 60% interest from viewers. The social media post can also be ranked in search engines, by incorporating hashtags and keywords.

- Provide variety

In a saturated niche, creating unique content can be a challenge. However, you have your own personality, and you have your own goals. Use your inspirations to publish something that people can relate to. At the same time, it must be unique and free from plagiarism. There's no limit to how creative you can be in the digital world. Think of every social media post as a picture. Paint it with your colors and the things that your brand's prospects need from you.

That, too, could convey more than a thousand words. Consider every word as an opportunity to make you stand out from the crowd. And create a one-of-a-kind content. In the following sections, you can learn the secrets to providing relevant and unique content.

- Entertain

Entertaining social media content isn't exactly pet tricks or slapstick.

This kind of digital content could be intriguing, interesting, or educational. If it entertains, consumers will likely make the effort to look for more posts from you. They may like your page and spend more time browsing your albums. In the upcoming chapters, you can learn how to create and publish entertaining public posts. With such a skill, you can prompt users to learn more about your service or product.

- Inspire

Inspiring quotes and images of phrases encourage reactions, which could be heart emojis, likes, or comments. Whether it's a clickable link to a sales page or a call-to-action for a product page, your SMM content must inspire them to do something--make an action.

Also, they must feel something about it. It must stir their insides and evoke emotion. An effective SMM strategy connects a brand with its audience. You can do this by providing inspirational content. Once you've built a great following, you need to remain relevant, keep engaging your loyal followers, and connect with prospects.

Many fail to maintain stability, and by changing their brand image, they tear down the loyalty and positive image they've built over time. For example, Jazza, a Youtuber and freelance artist, has millions of subscribers on YouTube. His viewers and subscribers grew due to his fun way of presenting drawing lessons. Over the years, Jazza provided different entertaining videos related to art, from sculpting lessons to funny and goofy art videos.

Although he was able to entice younger generations, many were also unsubscribing from his channel. In 2019, several of his avid viewers have expressed their reasons "why" and their sentiment that Jazza's channel is slowly becoming a channel for kids. The creator did indeed become popular due to his straightforward and easy art lessons.

The majority of his old subscribers made most of the views in his old videos. Between 2018 and 2019, the number of views in his channel declined and many people unsubscribed. They didn't appreciate Jazza's funny videos.

Staying relevant may sound challenging especially in the digital age, wherein internet icons are sprouting as fast as mushrooms. Nevertheless, the answer to this common dilemma is simple! You must regularly generate content that consumers/followers/viewers/prospects will crave for and relate to.

By getting personal and tapping into their interest, you can greatly connect with your fans. For instance, you can publish posts that show happy people embracing nature or pursuing their passions. You can take advantage of such scenarios and incorporate what your product/service can offer.

Subconsciously and succinctly, convey to your audience that a product of yours is what fuels the positive emotions in the image. This form of content marketing strategy creates rapport. It can even form bonds with consumers even after a purchase has been made. This can happen if you really provide a "quality" product.

☐ Make Your Content Scannable

The majority of social media users and searchers on the web hate blocks of text. People view texts and images differently online than in print. While they'll consume magazine articles completely, web surfers tend to have short attention spans and most of them are always in a hurry to find the information they need.

That's why a blog or social media post is more effective if it's scannable. Use bullets and numberings to help readers find what they're looking for fast. Break up walls of texts into easily digestible paragraphs. Avoid writing fluff--words, phrases, and sentences that are irrelevant to the topic. And keep paragraphs short and straightforward.

Write clearly and succinctly. You can throw in a complex sentence from time to time. But let your reader's rest. Too many complex and compound sentences in succession can be confusing. Let them pause with a short sentence before throwing in another compound sentence. Nevertheless, you must still avoid monotonous sentences one after another.

Successive complex or simple sentences can also kill the flow and grace of your content.

- ☐ Include an Intriguing Title

For articles and video content, you don't need to write click-baits, misleading, and scandalous headlines in order to attract viewers/readers. In fact, the majority of internet surfers hate click-baits. Once they know that the content is different from the title, they will feel fooled and frustrated. Often, they unfollow the creator of videos with clickbaits.

The World Wide Web is full of fluff. How can you make people read your offers and engage with your content? You need more high-quality content and great visuals to achieve such goals. What you need the most is a good headline. The title, meta title, or headline of your article is the hook and the eye-catcher of your entire piece.

The same principle can be applied to blogs, books, and social media posts. Focus on your chapter and write something that is as irresistible as a cute cat meowing. Try to put yourself in the reader's shoes, and ask yourself, "Would my title make me want to read on?"

If it doesn't, then refrain from publishing your post yet. Concentrate on your title in order to garner more love, more likes, and more shares! You must hook your audience. To do this, write headlines and subheadings that tell readers why your content is worth their precious time.

You can use the valuable tips below whenever you want to write a powerful title, subject, or headline.

- ✓ Keep it short and straightforward

- ✓ Clearly write the benefit of your content
- ✓ Announce relevant and exciting news that your audience cares about
- ✓ Ask questions
- ✓ Appeal to those who crave data, information, and knowledge
- ✓ Guide your audience and tell them what to do
- ✓ Show through writing that you offer the most valuable information source
- ✓ Use words and phrases like "101," "an introduction," "a beginner's guide to," "all you need to know," "everything you need to know," "now you can have," etc.
- ✓ Promise something audacious, like "you can grow hair in just 3 days."
- ✓ Use "how," "why," "what," or "when"
- ☐ Publish compatible content

You must always make sure that the content can be viewed and be read easily across many devices, including smartphones and mobile tablets. Nowadays, many people surf the web and open their social media on their smart devices. It won't do well for you if your digital media or blogs aren't mobile-friendly.

- ☐ Publish regularly

Now, you know how to create profitable SMM content and how to publish one. There is still a lot to learn like "taking advantage of social media features" and "scheduling and using a marketing calendar."

The other SMM necessities, like using hashtags and optimizing images and videos for SEO, are further tackled in the following sections and chapters. Plus, please keep in mind that your avid followers look forward to regular content from you. By neglecting posting schedules, social media platforms will stop recommending your posts to online followers.

For example, if you have made it a habit to post motivational quotes on your business FB page every Wednesday. Your page's regular readers will stop by every Wednesday to check out your new content. If you neglect this, you may lose the rapport you've painstakingly built.

Optimizing Videos, Images, and Podcasts

Since search engine giants can't parse multimedia contents, you've to use relevant keywords in every <alt> tag, metatag, or descriptive field. Make sure that these fields are content-rich and keyword-rich.

How can you do that? This section is exactly just for that. Since at this point you understand keyword research, you can recycle the relevant search terms in your blog and site contents. You may also use the introduction you've created and some optimized texts.

However, avoid too much duplication. Make sure that not at least three consecutive words are similar to your original copy. You can further optimize your digital medias by following the tips below:

- ☐ Filenames

Using filenames capture1511.jpeg or recording.AAV doesn't help in search engine optimization. Names like ChrismasPlushiesSale.jpg or PetCareFood.mp4 are way more helpful. Also, use the dash sign as a replacement for spaces. Take the following filenames as an example:

- ✓ Foods-for-Senior-Cats.jpg

- ✓ How-to-optimize-social-media-posts.mp4
- ✓ Pizza-Shop-LA.jpg
- ☐ Long-tail metatags

Long-tail metatags are keyword phrases with more than four words. If you're opting for a long-form copy or a lengthy social media post, you should use long-tail keywords. The most effective tags are in question form. They're quite effective for eCommerce and product marketing.

- ☐ Content

Surround your multimedia with unique and keyword-rich content. Don't forget to include keywords and search terms in the caption fields.

- ☐ Anchor text

Although incorporating anchor texts can boost the results of your SEO efforts, doing so can annoy users. After clicking an image and they're redirected to another site, they may think that your social media page or website is infested with advertisements.

That's why you must only use images with anchor texts sparingly. Only insert anchor texts if the redirected page provides more information about the topic. Do this when the website is related to the image's message.

- ☐ Transcription

For video files, transcribe, edit, and post a short excerpt from the media's content. This bear excellent results on YouTube. The search bots will be able to scan the post faster if a short part of the video has been converted into text.

- ☐ Large images

Upload images with high resolutions. You must also upload the large versions of the thumbnails visible on your social channel, website, or blog. If you won't, the thumbnails may appear grainy and pixelated. On the web, low-quality visuals spell lacks care and experience. According to SproutSocial, the majority of surfers ignore pixelated images and thumbnails. This is true for both search engine surfers and social media users.

☐ XML and RSS

You can expand your reach on social media with site maps and RSS.

RSS stands for Really Simple Syndication. It's a format utilized for publishing news-worthy content, such as news, headlines, and blogs. For consistency, each RSS feed looks the same.

Typically, RSS includes a teaser, title, and body text. It may also include the name of the author and the publishing date. RSS feeds display the latest entries first. Nevertheless, the total number of entries varies.

By incorporating RSS feeds to your published posts, your prospects can subscribe to your news feeds and receive a notification every time you post something new. If you produce delectable and high-quality content, the headline and your name or brand will appear on the subscriber's personal computer or mobile phone.

Without expenses, the content is delivered as push notifications upon posting. That's the power of RSS feeds. Aside from the aforementioned benefits, here are eight more ways you can use RSS feeds in social media marketing:

- ✓ Create newsletters with ease
- ✓ Distribute blog content
- ✓ Utilize the feeds for conceptualizing future posts/tweets

- ✓ Be able to recognize proper LinkedIn questions
- ✓ Track-specific Google searches
- ✓ Search for Quora topics related to your keywords

Overall, RSS feeds allow you to easily push content on social media.

Now, it's time to discuss XML. What is it exactly? XML stands for Extensible Markup Language. It defines the set of standards for encoding documents. The format is for humans and machines. This implies it's both machine-readable and human-readable.

By utilizing XML, organizations can parse data, including personal information and web and social media content, in various ways.

For indexing results, search engine giants greatly rely on their spider bots to scan the World Wide Web. Scanning and indexing transpire in milliseconds. Nevertheless, you can still increase your site speed and the duration it takes for crawlers to scan your pages and website.

This is where an XML sitemap becomes handy. Despite being just a file, it guides the crawlers to what to look for on your website.

Hence, it can also tell the bots to avoid a specific page or to focus on a specific group of entries.

An XML sitemap looks something like the image below:

In the example, the sitemap has one link. There are 3 required parts in XML sitemaps. The first one is the "<urlset>." This contains all the URLs of the chosen pages.

The second part is the <url> tag. This serves as the container of all the data related to the included URLs.

Inside the <url> tag is the (<loc>) or the location tag. There, you must put all the links of all the pages you want the spider bots to crawl. However, if you include the following, the bots may shy away from your content.

- The (<lastmod>) or the last modification tag tells when is the last modification of a specific file.

- The (<changefreq>) or the change frequency tag provides the data for the frequency of updates of each page.

- The (<priority>) or the priority tag tells the bots which web pages are the most important on your site.

How to Create a Branded Hashtag

Today, online businesses use hashtags to make their brand searchable on the web. Doing this enables them to serve information about their product to the right audience. Whether it's a term, branded phrase, or call-to-action, a branded hashtag enables internet surfers to find and connect with your business.

You may have already seen the Twitter hashtag #ShareaCoke or #YesWeCan. Despite sounding casual, they're examples of branded hashtags that have gone viral.

Branded hashtags can start as a campaign slogan and then become a viral term on social platforms. However, you need to research before launching your brand's hashtag so that your marketing efforts will bear good results.

To give you a headstart, here's a guide for creating a business hashtag that has the potential to go viral.

1) Firstly, make a list of all the tags or keywords relating to your brand. This includes the slogans you often use.

2) Second, search the hashtag on IG, TikTok, Twitter, and YouTube so that you can be sure that no one has come up with it yet. Yes, it must be original. You must also check if the hashtag isn't used for something undesirable.

3) Next, use the hashtag in your tweets, on your website, and other social channels. If you can, you should also edit your old posts and past articles and then include the hashtag at the bottom of each post or in the body of the content.

4) To make your followers get accustomed to your chosen branded hashtag, include the hashtag in your digital media, Twitter bio, pinned tweet, ad packaging, and PowerPoint presentations.

Once your followers and consumers start to become familiar with the tag, they might use it as well when tweeting about you, your brand, your product/service, or anything related to your page.

Usually, users utilize hashtags to search for their favorite brands on Twitter, TikTok, and Instagram. After you've amassed loyal followers, they'll use your hashtag on their posts when showcasing your product to the world or whenever they desire to interact with you.

Hence, you must always check the hashtag on the platform you've chosen.

Having a branded hashtag is also the easiest way to know the preferences, personalities, and pain points of your followers and consumers. With it, you can promptly react and respond to their posts, tweets, and inquiries.

According to TrackMaven, longer hashtags, which include keywords relevant to a particular niche/industry, are better than shorter ones. However, if you plan to use a long branded social media tag, it must be easy to spell and remember. Also, avoid using confusing terms and weird abbreviations.

Once you've come up with a branded hashtag, start using it on all of your posts, contents, sites, blogs, and materials related to your business. In addition, you can give your followers instructions or short guides for hash-tagging their posts.

Do you know what's best for popularizing a hashtag? Plan and host a contest or giveaway. By doing so, many people will enthusiastically use your brand's hashtag. Your product, as well as your brand, could go viral! And you'll gain new followers and reach new prospects.

By spending a few bucks or sacrificing some of your time, you can improve your brand's online exposure and have it exposed to many prospective customers. During the contest or promotion period, regularly check the hashtag often.

You can do this by tapping the hashtag itself. Then, you can see all the profiles that have used the hashtag. Also, by doing this, you can monitor conversations, engage with them, and build rapport with old and new consumers.

Actually, this is also a form of lead generation. For example, Twitter users check your tweet about the contest, engage with it, follow the instructions, and join the other users. That's why it's very important to write clear and concise introductions.

Remember, Twitter only allows 160 characters in every tweet. In one tweet, you must include that participants need to "follow" your page, "like" a specific number of tweets, and "retweet" the post. The more people that become leads and engage with your post, the more impressions and new followers your profile gets.

☐ On some social platforms, you can go viral hours after creating an account

For example, your tweet on Twitter can go viral even if you're just a new Twitter user. However, this is only possible if you know how to make viral tweets.

Anyone who regularly utilizes social networking platforms can view many viral tweets, daily. Such posts can come from anyone, even from those who originally just have ten followers.

Brands can also go viral with just a tweet. That's just one way of making viral social media posts. In the next chapters and sections, you can learn the other ways.

☐ Follower insights can help you develop your social media persona

The more you know about your fanbase or your brand's target audience, the better it is for your brand. Having a social media persona enables you to design a meaningful social strategy for capturing the attention and hearts of your leads. With an excellent brand persona, you can publish tweets that resonate with prospects.

Do you know what your ideal customer literally looks like? In this day and age, people, especially those that surf the web for their needs, crave personalization. In other words, they prefer relatable brands. Hence, it will pay off to define your customer base and create a brand persona just for them.

However, when you're looking at hundreds and thousands of followers, how can you guarantee your brand message and business goals are on point? If this has been bugging your mind, then welcome to the world of social media marketing.

Having a marketable personality, lets you wear a proverbial mask while at the same time being able to show your fun and quirky side. This may sound unprofessional, but this is how internet icons become viral and popular.

Such folks know who to impress and what to express. Besides, you can easily form bonds with people who are quite similar to you.

With the sheer amount of free customer data, you can gather via social media and by using free analytics tools, such as Snaplytics and BuzzSumo, knowing more about your fanbase and the general audience is as easy as turning on a personal computer. You just need to know-how.

☐ Further defining "social media persona"

What exactly is a social media persona? It's a fictional representation of your brand's ideal customer. It's also similar to your brand persona. Your brand's persona is what prospects and loyal customers perceive of the person behind the brand, which could be you or whoever created the brand. It exudes the will, aim, or virtue of the brand/business/company owner in question.

By considering elements in social media analytics, like desires, demographics, and pain points, you're slowly, but surely, painting a general image of the people you're trying to attract or sell to. In conclusion, a social media persona is the profile of the perfect customer for your brand.

When creating a brand persona, you need to find the answer to the following questions:

- ✓ What is the gender of the customer? Or do you cater to both sexes?
- ✓ What is his/her demographic?
- ✓ What age range does he/she belong to?
- ✓ In what country/state/region does he/she reside?
- ✓ Does he/she belong to your niche?
- ✓ What are his/her preferences and personality? Is she a chick kind of person? Or does he value minimalism?

Those are just some of the questions you must consider. Perhaps, your audience is mainly composed of baby boomers or Millennials.

For example, the brand "Denny" is known online for its meme-heavy content. Such posts are loved by millennials, craving for humor. Nevertheless, Denny's FB page caters to older crowds. There, they publish formal-style ads, yet their FB posts also receive high engagement.

Obviously, the brand has created different social media persona on the two platforms. With this kind of marketing strategy, they can speak and interact with multiple customer bases. And they're capable of crafting different types of content for both demographics.

By defining social media personas, you can target the best customers for your brand and craft tailor-made content for them.

Plus, having a social media persona enables you to design compelling ads that answer specific needs and wants.

- ☐ Tapping into profitable audience and prospects

In whatever niche or industry, you're in, online competition is fierce. That's why it's best to tap into niche markets before you launch your business.

Rather than opting for the traditional trickle-down approach, you should target a specific type of people. Refrain from chasing just anyone and everyone. Your social media persona will tell you who they are and where they flock online.

The brand Overtone has defined its social media persona well. Although the brand is presented as your everyday beauty brand, their loud feeds and colorful ad campaigns primarily attract working-class millennial women and young adults. The high level of engagement they garner on Twitter and Instagram is no accident.

How to Create a Social Media Persona

When crafting a social media persona, the most common pain points and baseline metrics for consideration are listed below:

- ✓ Goals for using the web
- ✓ Search intent
- ✓ Goals for using the social platform
- ✓ Brands they fancy
- ✓ Objections
- ✓ Personality traits
- ✓ Frustrations/Pain points

- ✓ Spending power/Income
- ✓ Age and gender
- ✓ Location, race, and culture

From social media metrics to data considered as subjective, such as frustrations and preferences, are all available to you with just a few clicks. For example, you can know the performance of each tweet you make by clicking the bar chart icon under each tweet.

Social listening and monitoring allow you to know the "preferences of your audience. You may even uncover shared concerns and similar interests. If this does happen, you'll have the opportunity to easily connect with your target audience.

For starters, identify your top-performing posts and determine when the content has been published. By doing this, you can publish similar tweets and make uploads during the "best times." The best times are the timeframes when most of your target "followers" and "prospects" are online on the platform.

Additionally, you may also gather information from LinkedIn, Twitter Analytics, and Facebook Insights. Looking at the individual profiles of proponents, loyal customers, and possible prospects can also help in painting the ideal social media persona for your brand.

-Integrating Your Social Media Personas into Your Marketing Plan

You have now defined your persona, so it's time to put it into action. You've all the data you need. What will you do with it? Here's a step-by-step guide to getting started.

1) Segment your audience

While creating personas, you will realize that your customers have many faces. This means that although they may belong to the same location and classification, they still have different personalities.

This step can influence everything from your ad strategies to your content calendar. For example, Facebook ads enable you to design advertisements based on audience variations. You need to ensure that your marketing calendar includes posts that don't overlook important characteristics of your brand's social media persona or buyer persona.

2) Integrate your brand voice

Once you integrate your brand voice, you'll have more meaningful conversations with your followers. Knowing what tone to use will allow you to adapt to the mood of the person you're having a conversation with. Then, you'll find it easier to converse with your other fans.

Brand voice influences ad copy and social captions. For example, Chewy, a manufacturer of pet toys and kibbles, has mastered a playful, distinct brand voice for their animal-loving audience.

Integrating your brand voice will make you stand out among your competitors.

3) Tweak your marketing strategy

In this step, you need to consider how the personas affect your content strategy. Your tweets—your content--must speak to the frustrations and motivations of your brand's social media persona.

By responding to comments or providing a particular type of content, how can you help your followers reach their goals? Please take note of the following tip:

Whether it's your next live video or blog post, you must always know what your personas are buzzing about every single day. That's why attention to detail and social listening are very important.

4) Reframe your content based on the customer's perspective

Too often, marketers use jargons and corporate speak that are meaningless to customers and prospects. If your audience can't understand what you say, it will be hard to connect with them.

Social media personas allow you to focus on addressing the needs of your prospects other than your own. Social media marketing is all about boosting sales while developing trust and brand loyalty.

5) Use social ads

This step is optional. If you want to go all organic, then please proceed to the next step. But, if you choose to include paid advertising to your marketing plan, you can create very targeted ads that can speak to your audience. By using social targeting and paid ads, you can get your tweets and content in front of the right people.

Create separate content for each of your social media personas. This is an advanced level of targeting. It improves social campaigns and increases conversion rates.

6) Increase return on investment (ROI) with a buyer persona spring

Developed by authors and professors Gordon Fletcher, Aleksej Heinze, Ana Cruz, and Tahir Rasid, the buyer persona spring allows you to connect business objectives. Why is it referred to as a spring? This is because it refers to three distinct loops:

☐ Data

Good data enables you to monitor reports and results. It allows you to revise your strategy accordingly.

☐ Channels

Determining the most used channels by your social media personas is as important as tweaking your paid advertisements.

☐ Content

What kinds of digital content will make your buyers connect with you. For example, the majority of Millennials like memes and colorful visuals.

Each of the above parts of the buyer persona spring includes four points. They are *act*, *plan*, *reflect*, and *observe*.

7) Compiling data on your existing customers and followers

To compile the data of your customers, you need data for the following demographics:

- ✓ Life stage
- ✓ Challenges
- ✓ Interests
- ✓ Spending patterns and spending power
- ✓ Language
- ✓ Location
- ✓ Age

You can do this manually, which might take some time. But opting for this bears more accurate results. Or you can use analytics tools like the following:

- ✓ Google Analytics
- ✓ Keyhole
- ✓ Curalate
- ✓ Snaplytics
- ✓ BuzzSumo

- ✓ TapInfluence
- ✓ SproutSopcial

If you're into business-to-business (B2B) marketing aside from SMM, you must also consider the size of the business you're representing, as well as its reach and the purchasing decisions of its prospects.

8) Learning about the social channels being used by prospects

You need to reach your prospective buyers on the right channel. Make sure that they're really on Twitter, and there should be a lot of them. Certain groups of people use the same social media platform. There will always be several of your prospects on a specific platform, but you need to focus your marketing endeavors on social media where most of them are active, on a daily basis.

Tools, like Keyhole and Hootsuite Insights, enable you to easily find the top authors, hashtags, and internet icons relevant to your brand and industry.

The last stage of this step is checking out the competition. You can use the aforementioned social tools for conducting competitor research.

9) Identifying customer pain points

You've just reached the most important part of this guide. In fact, without identifying the problems of your prospects, your marketing campaign will be as bland as a saltless porridge. It might be consistent, but that consistency will not go anywhere.

Once you have the demographics listed down, as well as the preferences of your customers and future clients, you can clearly define their pain points. What daily hassles or life problems are your prospects facing? What are their desires? Do you think your brand can cater to their needs? If so, how can you aid them?

There are two ways you can know the answers to such questions. You've to engage in sentiment analysis or social listening.

By setting up search streams, you can monitor mentions of your competitors, products or services. Doing this provides a real-time view of the trends in the industry and what users are saying about your brand online. You can learn important insights, like what they love about you and what they need from your business.

10) Identifying customer goals

This is the opposite of knowing customer pain points, but they're equally important. As much as you need to know about your prospect's problems, you must also consider their drive, goals, and aspirations.

By doing so, you'll have the ability to entice them to fulfill your own set marketing goals. You must research more about their personal preferences and other positive things they desire to achieve.

Their goals could be professional or personal. It's up to you to discover what are those. These must be related to the solutions you're offering, or rather, their goals must be matched to the benefits and features of your product. If these are different with the goals of your prospects, then you can't consider them as your leads.

Social listening is an excellent way to gather data about the preferences, personalities, and aspirations of your prospects. If you own a BPO or advertising firm, your CS team can provide valuable insights for formulating pain points. Your sales team, on the other hand, is a good source for knowing your customer's goals.

Your sales team talk to genuine purchasers. They know about the complaints and enthusiasm of some of your brand's verified clients.

Overall, if your sales team has interacted with many types of clients/customers, then it will be much easier for you to formulate the best social media persona for the brand you're handling. Also, don't forget to ask your markers to gather real quotes.

11) Understand how you can provide solutions

Once you know the necessary goals and pain points, you can proceed to visualizing interactions wherein you're answering the needs of your prospects. In this step, you must analyze deeply how your customers can benefit from your brand. After this, you can create your social media persona.

12) Creating the persona

You have the data you need, so you can now look at the common characteristics of your brand's clients. Once you group the characteristics, you can form the basis of the unique social media personas.

For example, you identify a group of fathers between the age of 30 to 40. They live in big cities and they 're fond of camping. They also own minivans. Now, you must make use of that abstract collection of data and use it as a basis of your brand's social media persona.

Give the persona a home, job title, and name. It needs to be like an authentic person, and in this step, you must also include the goals and pain points of your customers. In the example above, the group of city dads who are fond of camping can be represented by a persona named George.

Based on your social research, George, the representative of the group, has the following characteristics.

- ☐ He's a middle-aged salaryman.
- ☐ He probably has 2 to 4 kids.
- ☐ He lives in Miami, Florida.
- ☐ He owns 1 to 4 automobiles.

- ☐ He's fond of camping throughout Florida.
- ☐ His vacation time is very limited.

The list can go on and on. That's why you need to prioritize the most important characteristics, like age, address, and hobbies. Not all people in the group will match the buyer persona. Nevertheless, it represents the group to you and enables you to consider them more humanly.

It's much easier to talk to George compared to 40-year-old dads who own a mini-van. This allows you to think about how your services and products can serve your prospects. These are the members of the group that "George" represents.

Once you've crafted the ideal persona, you can proceed to employ free analytics.

For example, Twitter offers free social analytics. This doesn't require third parties, additional app download, or add-on installation. Its core feature—the Audiences tab--can help you visualize a picture of your average follower.

On this platform, Audiences have four categories: Lifestyle, Demographics, Mobile Footprint, and Consumer Behavior. The generated results provide insights into your follower's interests.

Brand Voice: Why You Need It, How to Craft One, and Integrating Your Brand Voice into Your Marketing Plan

Ask yourself, "What words do your friends and loved ones use when describing you?" In their eyes, are your kind, witty, or helpful?

Now, which words will you use to describe your brand? If you're finding it hard to answer this question, then you definitely need to develop your brand's voice. If you don't have an answer right now, you need to craft one, fast!

Remember, the voice of your brand represents your business' goals, virtue, and personality.

Social media persona is a visualization of your brand's ideal customer, while brand voice should be the message your prospect perceives. This message must be able to turn them into leads and put your brand under a good light.

Your brand's personality--its voice—needs to be steady and consistent. This is very important for your social media marketing strategy. Markets that rely on the web for making a profit and generating leads are all heavily saturated, nowadays. This means that competition is extremely rife, even in your niche.

Yes, the competition is very extreme! It seems that budding brands won't have a place under any of the spotlights. If there's no opportunity, then why not create one?

Your brand needs to stand out. In a saturated niche, digital content often looks and feels the same. That's why you must establish your brand as something different from the rest. Whether you opt to publish funny content or helpful guides, your brand must make a name for itself.

Developing a brand voice is an effective way to stand out like a red mushroom among a sea of green moss. Once you've crafted one, stick with it and avoid confusing your readers.

Kate Spade, an American entrepreneur and fashion designer, said, "Your voice must start with your brand's promise. It's your content and story, but it must start with your customer."

-Defining Brand Voice

Brand voice encompasses everything from the language and words you use, to the image and personality your social media page invokes. The voice of your brand should aim to cut through the noise in your niche and etch itself into the minds of your prospects.

-Why is it Important?

What do well-rooted companies have in common? Their purpose is clear, and they exude a strong voice and solid personality.

Brand voice and brand recognition go hand in hand. At the same time, Gaining the attention of consumers requires consistency. If you're messaging or personality often changes, it will be hard for your audience to understand your intention. It will be difficult for them to gauge whether you're friendly or untrustworthy.

As a consequence, your marketing efforts may bear poor fruits. Your consumers will instead choose the well-branded options. Even if you offer high-quality products, that won't do much for your business. You need to tell your audience just that.

With your brand voice, you can tell your audience that you've something up for grabs and that you're the entity that you claim to be.

-Tone vs. Voice

Crafting a brand voice and using tone in creating content for marketing are integral elements of branding. Both can help in improving online exposure and in making products or services stand out on any social media platform.

The longest-lasting and most beloved companies are those that have considered the importance of "taking the time to build their brand." They have invested both time and money in building a solid personality and consistent presence.

When consumers consider brands, they often choose those that they can relate to. That's why marketers focus on the business's online reputation and visual identity. Tone and voice are often overlooked.

Before you look at branding as a whole, you must consider those two elements and be able to differentiate one from the other. This is another issue in SMM and content marketing. Marketers and brand managers often think of tone and brand voice as two similar things.

Yes, they have similarities, but one is different from the other. Brand voice is your business' personality, which should be unchanging. Tone, on the other hand, is the emotional inflection the voice exhibits. The tone is meant to adjust to a specific kind of message or particular content type.

Inflection is the modulation in the form of a word or phrase. It expresses a grammatical attribute, which includes case, mood, tense, gender, person, and number.

While voice remains consistent, the tone should change according to each tweet's context. As an example, a tweet about an extreme sale for a product would sound more light-hearted than headline news that the company has published.

-Using Tone in Marketing

In truth, tone is everything in marketing. It could make or break your message, your brand, and your business.

Individuals who emit confidence and those who are bright and self-assured are people magnets. They attract people, unknowingly and subconsciously. Even with just a small gesture of kindness or by just sharing something funny, they can brighten up someone's day and inspire others to do something.

The same is true for brands and businesses that operate online. When branding, you also need to have an effective and influential tone that sounds authentic, not forced, on top of the incorporation of a solid brand voice.

It's now time to bring back the basics. You must be able to clearly define what makes a brand voice and how tone can be used to evoke emotions and catch the attention and hearts of your prospects.

Every heading on your website, every email, and tweet you send, or any piece of information you provide must exude the established voice of your business. Each content you publish should tell your brand's story while forming relationships and evoking a tone that could win the trust of prospects and make you more relatable.

Every single thing about tone and voice boils down to how you interact with your followers and prospects. The continuous development of a business' branding strategy and exposure and the engagement of loyal followers greatly relies on repetition and consistency.

Your audience will be confused when you constantly change your brand voice. Even if you have incorporated a relatable tone, a business that has too many faces would fail to meet its goals. You may get lesser likes and CTR than usual.

Keep in mind that your fanbase might've gotten used to a specific voice of yours. So, changing it would make them question your motive, as well as the underlying emotions behind the post and your real personality.

-Defining Tone and its Significance

For some, they'll never know the distinctions between tone and voice until they go deep into SMM or content marketing. Fortunately, you have this book with you.

For starters, try visualizing a sarcastic individual. This could be your friend or someone close to you. Don't look at the context of his message. Instead, take into account how he says her words.

Observe how he phrases the words and look at his facial expression. All of these are elements of his message's tone.

Consider yourself as an example too. How many times have had people misunderstand you?

In the past, you might have said something harmless, but you uttered it in an unusual way. And someone may misinterpret it, causing misunderstandings and wrong inferences.

You might have said, "Hey, bro you need to put on some weight." If you said this while smiling, the receiver might see it differently. Even if you had no bad intentions, your friend might think otherwise.

The same thing can be said when you're branding on social media. Just one wrong move and your reputation, which you might have built for years, can go down the drain.

For example, back in 2018, a gaming icon known for his helpful gaming tips for playing F2P, in the World of Warcraft (WoW), made a huge blunder. This revealed something undesirable about the player.

Before that happened, he had regularly posted in-game screenshots on Twitter. That time, he wrongly published the screenshots of his PVP victories. Before, his tweets had been well-received by his audience.

WoW, being a competitive online game, can be difficult to play. That's why that gamer was popular among many WoW players. For years, he had been providing helpful tutorials, gameplays, and walkthroughs to the community, until that fateful day.

He had a bad habit though. He edited his win rates and win counts. On that day, he tweeted the same content four times. He deleted the tweets because the images appeared misaligned after publishing. However, his followers could still see the tweets he had deleted that day. That time, he should've deactivated his Twitter account.

In one of the tweets, the gamer uploaded the raw, unedited, screenshot of his win rate. Because of this, his followers saw the differences. Because of his blunder, they saw through his veil and dishonesty. Many pointed out what he had done and almost all of his avid followers lost trust in him.

They even tried to make his edits go viral. You're pretty familiar by now with Twitter's "hashtag" feature, so you can imagine what happened to the gamer's online reputation. He lost many followings, and a hashtag was made in honor of his blunder. The hashtag was like a branded one, but its aim was to defame the gamer.

Truly, if done properly, tone could build trust with prospects and further improve brand exposure. However, just one wrong move could break your brand. When this happens, you'll be forced to assume a new online identity.

How to Use Tone More Effectively When Branding?

By incorporating the right tone in each of your social media post, you can create a trustworthy environment for your audience. Rather than sounding forced and superficial, you must breed trust and promote a sense of security. Then, your loyal followers will not hesitate to engage with you.

Social media users will more likely engage with you if you exude a friendly and trustworthy personality. However, this is only possible if you have developed such an environment in the digital world. For some, visiting a friendly and trustworthy profile is equivalent to having a respite.

For example, maintaining a consistent posting schedule allows your followers to know when to interact with your tweets. It's also best to post during the times when most of your prospects and leads are active online.

Chubbies is an example of a business that has effectively leveraged its unique brand voice. Chubbies mainly cater to male consumers. The brand is popular to backpackers, college students, and working bachelors. Here are some of the things that have contributed to their success.

- ✓ Chubbies knows who they are
- ✓ They know the type of people to impress and what market to focus their efforts on
- ✓ Their advertisement tone and brand voice reflect their business goals and virtue

In a recent interview, Rainer Castillo, Chubbies' co-founder, has made a noteworthy comment about modern marketing strategies. He said, "Over the years we've operated, we realized, along the way, that the success of our company has relied on one very important thing: treating customers as friends.

I think I could say that when you read our email newsletter, the tone of the message and how it has been written will make you say, 'Uncle Ben had written this email to a friend.' We make sure to not just sound friendly and casual, but to also be relatable and provide answers to our reader's pain point."

To figure out what tone will work best for your brand, take into consideration the following:

- ✓ Your target markets
- ✓ The industry and niche you're in
- ✓ The social media persona for your business
- ✓ Your planned posts
- ✓ Your services/products

What kind of marketing strategy or approach will increase engagement? Do you think your viewers will respond better with informal content or will they be irked by it? Will they prefer a professional or business-like tone? Perhaps, they would be engaged by something in between, like a conversational and informative article?

Chubbies, for example, targeted bachelors residing on college campuses. Their first followers were male college students who had enough friends, followings, and connections for them to become campus brand representatives.

Years ago, a happy and contented customer shared his positive experience with the brand. Because of Chubbies' casual and positive outlook, the consumer did not hesitate to reach out and express his circumstance.

The customer's car had been ransacked and all of his Chubbies items had been stolen. He was definitely a loyal customer of the brand. He tweeted images of his car's interior and shared what had happened.

The purpose of his tweet was to express his dismay, not to ask for compensation. Imagine your beloved collection robbed from you, never to be seen again. That's how he felt.

Chubbies sympathized with him on Twitter. The company then sent him new merchandise to replace everything that had been stolen from him. They even purchased karate lessons for the student so that he could defend himself and his stuff the next time someone would push him around.

That does sound heart-warming, doesn't it? The story would make you place the brand under a good light.

Chubbies' act of kindness had a marketing significance. It validated the founder's established goal of "treating customers like friends."

The company's actions look and feel special, authentic, and different.

In marketing, although "different tones resonate with different personas," the majority of people in the world are engaged by stories of kindness and those that exude positivity.

Chubbies did that to further prove their point and validate their virtue, goals, and intentions, online. It can be heart-warming to engage with a professional brand that seems friendly and reliable, especially when they reply!

If that's how you feel whenever you get a response from your social media idol, then why not do the same for your brand? Avoid sounding overly formal, avoidant, or cold to your followers. If they ask a question, respond to them. If they retweet your post or say something positive about your tweet, thank them. Treat them like how you would want to be treated. Like Chubbies, treat them as a friend!

However, always remember that your business tone must depend on the nature of your brand and your marketing plans.

Short Meaningful Activities for Developing a Brand Voice

When branding, beginner marketers often think about how a business looks visually. They often just focus on the logo, the headers and background wallpapers, and the design of the establishment. They often overlook the real meaning of brand voice.

In its simples form, brand voice is the emotion and personality infused into an entity's communications. It isn't just about the logo, or the profile picture being used. Rather, it's all about the goals and values of the company and the primary message it wants to convey.

The company who offers surf gears adapt the attitude and vocabulary of a surfer. The clothing company manufacturing preteen trendy clothes loosen its language and incorporate slang words into their informercials. These are just some worthwhile examples. To have a crafty brand voice for your brand, please follow the tips below:

☐ Review your brand's promise once again

This is the essence of your brand, but it isn't something that you need to outwardly say to your prospects or viewers. It remains as the foundation of how your brand promises to answer the market's issues/pain points and how it relates to customers.

If your brand can't promise anything, it will be difficult to formulate a brand voice and social media persona. Here are some excellent examples of brand promise from well-known brands.

- ✓ Walmart
- ✓ "Live better. Save money."
- ✓ Nike
- ✓ "We bring innovation and inspiration to athletes in the world."
- ✓ Apple
- ✓ "Think different."
- ✓ Coca-Cola
- ✓ "Inspiring uplifting and optimistic life moments."

With the examples above, you can say that brand promises are like taglines, which exudes the customer-centric goal of your business.

The promise is also an integral part of your content vision. Once it's set, you can develop a brand voice with ease. Try it!

- ☐ Purge and audit your existing tweets

You should do this if your social media page is quite old, or you've converted a personal profile into a business page. Handle and re-check all searchable

This includes old tweets, replies, and mentions. Search your old and current username both on Twitter and Google.

As much as you can, purge and remove irrelevant content. Remove anything that doesn't relate to your brand or any personal tweets that give a glimpse of other intentions, personal beliefs, or social life.

While auditing, purge content that doesn't represent your brand's promise. Despite outstanding marketing efforts, just one condemning tweet could affect online reputation.

This is quite similar to rebranding, which you should implement with caution. When rebranding, you can either assume a new brand voice and online persona, jump to another niche, or introduce content from a new genre.

Rebranding may sound easy, but if you don't do it right, it can hurt your brand and reputation on the web. In the last sections of this chapter, you'll learn how to properly rebrand a social media profile and know what to avoid.

Like brand voice, rebranding can make or break your business. For instance, if you are intending to assume a new online personality, your loyal followers may not recognize you and stop engaging with your tweets. Your new profile may appear as a total stranger to them.

In whatever you do online, do consider your audience. Their view and engagement with your account fuel your business to meet your set marketing goals.

☐ Ask your audience

According to Jeff Bezos, your brand is like what people say about you whenever you're not in the room. If your leads view your brand differently as you do, then you must properly implement a consistent brand voice.

Hence, you need to find out how your audience sees your brand. Then, reconcile your message with their perception of your social media profile. How can you do this?

Ask your followers questions by conducting surveys and polls. But avoid blatantly asking them about their views. Do it in a subtle way, like hosting a survey and offering prices to selected participants. By doing so, you can confirm whether or not your brand voice resonates with your audience.

Here are some sample questions you can include:

✓ Why sends hearts?

✓ Why avail of our services?

✓ What kind of content do you want to see more often?

Twitter offers a built-in feature that allows you to create and customize polls, surveys, and questionnaires.

☐ Create a tagline: describe your brand in just three words

If your brand or online persona is a human, what will you say about it? To answer this question, think of only three words? On Twitter, the number of characters you can use for your bio and tweets is very limited.

For tweets, only 160 characters are allowed, while you can just use 120 max characters for your bio. Using emojis and symbols can consume 3 to 5 characters.

Your goals, tagline, brand voice, and messages should be engaging, but they must be written clearly. Unlike Facebook, you can't write a whole essay or press release on Twitter.

That's why each message, each headline, and each tagline must promote clarity, uniqueness, and, most of all, conciseness. For your tagline or the very first words in your bio, make it a habit to only use three words.

Take the taglines below as examples:

- ✓ Research, Write, Deliver
- ✓ Bed and Breakfast
- ✓ Shave time and money
- ✓ Melts your tongue
- ✓ Just do it
- ✓ Got milk?
- ✓ Imagination at work
- ✓ Every little help
- ✓ Eat just one
- ✓ Play beyond reality
- ✓ We drive commerce

Now, why are taglines important? What's the relevance of a tagline in marketing? In a few words, a tagline can state and summarize a brand or a business' overall purpose. It lets leads and consumers alike sum up what you offer and what your brand is all about.

That's why taglines should be memorable. It could be a short phrase or a very short sentence, but it can deliver a great many things about your brand. For example, what do you infer from the tagline, "Work hard, play hard?"

Many people think that those who indulge in games and certain hobbies, like collecting stuff or binge-watching, are signs of irresponsibility and laziness. This is the reason why many freelancers hide their pastimes on social media and why people assume a different personality online.

Most employers frown upon the following habits: gaming and being a hobbyist. Recruiters tend to think that those who engage in such activities are lazy and disorganized. That's the stigma.

But what if you earn from being a gamer, by streaming your gameplays and creating content on YouTube and Twitch? Even though you're indeed a hobbyist or a gamer, you perform well in your job.

By using the tagline "work hard, play hard," you're conveying that you're a hard worker and that you deserve to enjoy a time to reward yourself for your efforts. That's the real message behind that tagline, although it could mean other things.

At the same time, you're also inspiring your followers to work hard too. If you're already well-rooted in your industry or have made a name in some online communities, many could be looking up to you, idolizing you.

However, that is only possible if you've properly connected with some of your followers. Making friends and forming bonds isn't only possible in real life, but in the virtual world as well. And friends are great sources of likes and other forms of online engagements.

In conclusion, taglines attract the right people, helping you create rapport. It also sets you apart from business rivals. On top of everything, you can use the first three words of your bio as the reference for all your future tweets. This helps you be consistent with your brand voice, even if you change your tone.

☐ Create and use a brand voice chart for future tweets

You're done with the three words for your bio, heading, and tagline. Now, start creating a chart with 3 columns. Dedicate a column for each word. You must create this chart in an excel sheet, notebook, or any writing medium that you can save for later.

Then, label the topmost rows with the following:

✓ Do

✓ Do not

✓ Description

For each word, write down what the "word" means to you under the "Description."

In the 2nd column, write the things you must do in order to fulfill what you've written in the description column. This part, including what you need to do for your brand to live up to the description.

Finally, in the do not column, list down the things you must avoid for your brand. For example, if you're managing a brand catering to gaming enthusiasts, avoid sharing rants and what you ate for breakfast.

When everything is taken into account, the purpose of the chart is to ensure that your brand voice remains consistent and true to your 3-word tagline.

If you say, "imagination at work" and your followers are used to seeing helpful gaming tips on your profile, then you suddenly talk about how your pet spilled ink all over your workplace. Do you think your audience will be able to relate to you?

Suddenly talking about an out-of-context topic can irk some people. You will look like an internet troll, but worse than that, you may lose respect and several followers.

☐ Look for inspiration, integrate your passion, and be inspired with the work

If you're new to SMM and brand voice development, you can look up to and study the marketing tactics of well-known brands in your niche. However, avoid blatantly copying them.

Some organizations appear snarky, while some are informative and respectful. Learn from their marketing tactics and content management, while providing unique content.

Here are some well-rooted firms with exceptional brand voices:

✓ Red bull
✓ MailChimp
✓ Wendy's

-Brand Voice Examples

You've just been acquainted with the fundamentals of creating a brand voice, as well as the best marketing tips for using a variety of tones in your content. In this section, you can refer to some real-world examples of exceptional brand voices.

The five examples below will answer your remaining questions about brand voice.

☐ MailChimp

Like other forms of digital marketing, email marketing has many intricacies that complicate it. But, with MailChimp's brand voice, they shout to the world that they can streamline the email marketing process.

Their headline simplifies their solutions. In a way, everyone can easily understand it. They can see the benefits offered by MailChimp, in just three words: helpful, warm, and welcoming.

- ☐ Duluth Trading Company

This trading firm specializes in manufacturing durable and appealing clothing for blue-collar workers. Their brand voice can easily explain their products' benefits.

In physical stores, signage reflects the store's views and the owner's personality. If you watch advertisements on TV, you can recognize your favorite brand immediately. This is largely due to their brand voice and tagline, which is often showcased at the end of the commercial.

Duluth leveraged this traditional marketing style. Although they often change their tone when introducing a different product, their brand voice remains consistent across all their products and subsidiaries.

Here's their universal brand voice: practical, irreverent, and authoritative.

- ☐ Apple

Almost everyone knows Apple and the creative mind behind it. This smartphone brand has sold more than 1.3 billion iPhones since 2007 and has toppled over well-rooted brands in the industry, like Nokia, BlackBerry, and Samsung. This figure doesn't include the cellphone enhancements and other merchandise the company has sold and circulated, over the years.

Since the company launched, its stock price has increased by 15%. In 2021, Apple is worth $1 trillion. This makes Laurene Powell Jobs, the widow of Apple's late co-founder, Steve Jobs, the 14th richest billionaire in the technology industry.

What has made this fairly young company to be one of the worlds biggest? The answer to that is their marketing strategy and brand voice: simple, clean, and confident.

Chapter End

The World Wide Web is full of fluffy and inaccurate content, which doesn't really provide value and solid information. By publishing texts and digital media that serve a particular purpose, you're not only improving the reputation of your brand, but you're also improving its reach while catering to the needs of your prospects. In the online world, you, your logo, and your brand will be recognized as a reliable and trusted source in your industry.

CHAPTER 3: MARKETING ON TWITTER AND USING THE PLATFORM AS A GATEWAY TO OTHER SOCIAL CHANNELS

Do you know when Twitter took the world by storm? Do you know how to leverage your social media accounts for your marketing strategies? In 2007, Twitter was launched.

At first, this social media platform was only embraced by blogging communities and casual SNS users. But, later on, marketers and brand managers started seeing its potential as a marketing tool and as an efficient medium for building rapport with loyal followers.

Like Facebook, Twitter is a user-friendly platform. This means it's very straightforward. Almost all functions are served on a silver platter. What you see is what you can get. There are no hidden settings or features, but many tips and strategies for becoming a successful Twitter marketer are kept secret.

This chapter will briefly discuss the benefits of Twitter as a marketing tool. The lessons in this chapter can teach you how to increase traffic and sales and earn passive income using the platform. And you will uncover many industry insights and marketing secrets for Twitter marketing.

Before you know it, you'll be sending tweets like an expert. For this to happen, you need to learn some Twitter etiquette first and know how to make the best use of the options, features, and opportunities that Twitter has to offer. As a valuable marketing tool, Twitter can make or break your brand.

Twitter Marketing at a Glance

Twitter and LinkedIn are perhaps two of the best platforms for finding clients, marketing opportunities, and freelancing jobs. If you aren't using this social media platform for reaching your prospects, you're missing out on a lot of opportunities and letting others grab them.

In case you don't know, you need to socialize where your leads are. Why do you've to socialize on Twitter? You'll soon find out. By being on this platform, you can start your small business on the right track.

According to CNBC, a world leader in business news and financial market coverage, approximately 80% of online jobs are posted on SNS mediums and are landed through networking. This means that the majority of clients, prospects, and recruiters aren't even using job boards. The importance of networks and social media in having a successful career stands to grow.

That is huge! Twitter offers 100% organic impressions. Unlike Facebook and Instagram, the active followers of your account and their followers can see your most recent post. This engagement opportunity is 100% free! On other social platforms, you need to pay for their ad's services, just to have all your online friends see your latest content.

According to Hootsuite, over 85% of B2B and B2C content marketers are operating on Twitter. And there are approximately 195 million daily active users on the platform. Undeniably, Twitter is an excellent social media network for finding leads, building links, and connecting with people and businesses.

Twitter is a virtual place where people can share their fleeting opinions and disseminate timely news, memes, and other types of content. From a perspective of a marketer, the social ecosystem of this SNS allows business owners to know what consumers want. They can leverage that information in order to create engaging and relevant content for their audience.

Business owners, as well as startups, should invest in Twitter, for the growth of their market and audience. As a marketer, you can use this social media platform to share valuable news in your industry and engage with your prospects. In 2020, Twitter has over 320 million monthly active users.

Although the figure is a bit lower than Facebook, Twitter offers a plethora of advantages (pros) that makes FB and IG look like expensive marketing platforms.

Offering free networking and analytics services and being one of the major social platforms in the world, Twitter is an indispensable SMM tool.

In truth, businesses, like Starbucks, HubSpot, and Sony PlayStation, market their brands on Twitter. Their goals are the same: boost conversions, increase brand awareness, and engage users and followers. What's more, Twitter streamlines the process of publishing relatable web content. The other pros are listed in the following section.

Twitter Statistics and Benefits for Marketers

- Twitter is popular in the USA, Japan, the UK, Saudi Arabia, and other first-world countries. As of 2020, Americans account for 33% of daily active Twitter users.
- In Japan, Twitter remains the number one social media.

- Approximately 35% of users on Twitter are women and the remaining 65% are men.
- In Q3 2019, Omnicore reported that about 55% of Twitter users earn $50,000 annually.
- On this social media platform, the most active users are millennials followed by boomers. 44% of Gen Z claims that they have a Twitter account. 21% of them report that they use the platform at least once per day.
- Twitter Agency Playbook, an American advertising agency managing Twitter ads, reported in 2019 that Twitter users watch 26% more advertisements than other user bases.
- Every day, almost 2 billion videos are watched on the platform.
- Twitter is considered the number one platform discovery. This is mainly due to its educated and influential audience.
- What's the best part of Twitter? Its marketing analytics tools. Despite being top-quality, the tools are free!
- This SNS platform provides many 2-way communication functions. With some of this feature allows you to directly interact with your followers.
- Unlike other social media platforms, Twitter allows you to combine both paid and organic searches.
- The platform is also well-suited for timely campaigns. Twitter can efficiently deliver real-time news, promos, and updates.
- For better productivity, take advantage of Twitter's Marketing Calendar and Events Dashboard. Both are free marketing tools that are exclusively available on the platform.

- You can facilitate networking with influencers and experts in your niche. Twitter upholds community building and professional networking. With its hashtagging feature, these are all possible.

- Staying active on the platform increases your chances to appear on Google's top ten, for a particular keyword. Google indexes Twitter posts too.

- When you include keywords and hashtags, your brand's prospects will see you. Twitter suggests posts with relevant tags and phrases to the users who usually engage with such content. These users are your prospects.

- With the search tool, you can check what your followers and consumers say about your brand. You can also search public posts by keyword.

- 58% of Twitter users report that they have a positive experience on the platform, in terms of making direct purchases.

- You can also use Twitter for monitoring the activities of your business rivals. Have they gone viral? You can check that out on Twitter as well.

- According to HubSpot, Twitter is the most user-friendly social media. Twitter can be easier to use than Facebook, Pinterest, and Instagram.

How to Make Money on Twitter?

For some users, Twitter isn't just a simple social channel where people can share, learn, and interact with others. It's also a virtual place where one can build a circle of friends, boost one's popularity, or be entertained. In truth, these all serve as the platform's foundations.

However, some see Twitter beyond all of its basic offerings and fundamental services. Some people create, develop, and improve their Twitter account, in order to earn money. Twitter is undeniably a good tool for generating passive income. But this is only possible if one knows how to do it properly.

To help you get started, here are some ways for using the platform. These can help you launch your first passive income campaign.

☐　Using Affiliate Marketing

The number of people on social apps and websites have been increasing rapidly. Nowadays, most marketers, freelancers, and business owners build their brands and businesses in the digital world.

That means, most digital brand owners want their products/services to flourish across the web. This is where affiliate marketing becomes profitable.

Affiliate marketing is considered a marketing strategy. It's also a type of passive income where one can earn through commission sales. It's a type of performance-based marketing, in which a brand rewards the affiliate for each lead they've converted.

There are many ways to design an affiliate marketing plan on Twitter. The easiest among them is *the use of third parties*, like Clickbank, Amazon Associate, FlexOffers, and many others.

Just make sure to take the time to research your choices first. There are hundreds of third-party advertising websites out there. You must know whether your choice is legit or not. You must be vigilant of scam websites.

Most brands have specific standards over their affiliate marketer applicants. Some companies require an account on Twitter that has at least 10,000 followers. This is why it's best to focus first on growing your Twitter following, before sending your application.

☐ Using Sponsored Tweets

Next on the list is *using Sponsored Tweets*. Just like an affiliate post, a sponsored tweet has to do with another brand/business/company. Both the marketer and the owner gain benefit. But how does a sponsored tweet work?

Commonly, influencers have a ready-made micro-content for their marketers. Having said that, you can think that, depending on the personality, expertise, or industry of a specific marketer, the micro-content would change.

For example, gender sets boundaries over the type of product that an influencer could receive from a brand. For female cosmetics, the brand representative would probably choose a female influencer.

In a sponsorship, the greatest role is played by the influencer. The brand garners its needed sales and engagement. On the one hand, the influencer receives compensation. This could be a product or payment. With this, it's evident that becoming an influencer is another great way to earn more money. You can sell the products that you get for free.

☐ Building an email list

Like YouTube, Twitter is an excellent place in the virtual world for finding emails. How can you get those sweet email addresses? Most business accounts showcase their emails in their bio or turn prospects into leads.

✓ Embed links on your tweets and bio

✓ Make tweets shareable

✓ Make your pinned tweets count and leverage and optimize the post

- ✓ Use content to drive them to your website where they can sign-up for your newsletters

- ✓ Build relationship with people and politely ask for their email through direct messaging

With an email list, you can foster trust and get customers to come back for more. You can also sell the emails. Every 100 working emails cost $12 to $80. The price depends on your industry and niche.

- ☐ Engage, build rapport, and sell

At its core, Twitter is a social platform. Its main purpose is to connect people. Time and time again, consumers turn to brands that they can trust. They patronize fellow users that they've deemed friendly and trustworthy.

Twitter, with its features, capabilities, and 100% engagement, is undeniably an excellent platform for creating rapport online, for going viral, and for sell anything.

So, here's the million-dollar question: how can you build relationships on this platform? To find the answer, please take a look at the following tips:

- ✓ Provide valuable information in your tweets

- ✓ Publish compelling and eye-catching tweets to boost the interest and engagement of your audience. For example, memes may look informal, but millennials love funny posts.

- ✓ Find and follow users who could be interested in your products, campaign, or services. You should particularly target influencers and experts. Their followers can be your leads too.

- ✓ To increase the impressions of your tweets, use hashtags and keywords.

- ✓ Always exude warmth and friendliness. A warm personality is friendly. Also, show enthusiasm and affection in your behavior, at all times.
- ✓ If the situation calls for it, you may ask your followers to retweet your post. Include this request in the tweet.
- ✓ Show gratitude to everyone who retweets and helps you spread the name of your brand. You can thank them in the comment section. Give simple rewards or mention their "@" handle on your timeline.

What are the Pros and Cons of Using Twitter?

Launched in 2006, Twitter was originally just a message board. Since then, the platform has grown into one of the world's largest social networks. 2020reports by Statistica show that 65% of online businesses use Twitter for advertising. Here are the advantages they've been enjoying since they started using this marketing platform:

☐ DMs create genuine connections

On Twitter, DM stands for direct messaging. Like its competitors, this social network provides a direct messaging feature, which enables private communications between two users. However, there's a catch. The two accounts must be mutual with each other.

Nevertheless, if the account is fairly new or the other user has set his/her account to "open," then you can contact that particular person. This may seem like a hindrance when contacting notable and popular industry players and prospective clients but reserving this feature for your "mutuals" assures you that communications will be personalized and worthwhile.

☐ The "tagging" feature encourages engagements

Twitter's "@" symbol provide many marketable opportunities. It's a gold key for sending notifications to other users, using your own Twitter brand. This almost guarantees that your post will be seen by the recipient. In addition to that, it's an easy way to attribute an article or a quote to someone.

A few years ago, Twitter has upgraded its Content Discovery function. With this, users are able to see tweets from profiles they don't follow. They can see the tweets their followers have liked.

The more people like and interact with your tweet, the more impressions it will get. Twitter scripts guess that the user may want to see tweets from pages they might fancy.

This is especially true when the user in question tends to interact with content similar to what you offer. With this, your viral tweets and those with high engagements will appear in front of prospective consumers. And thus, your online engagement and reach will greatly improve.

Soon, you'll learn more about Twitter's algorithms and the ways for outsmarting them.

- Most Twitter users value the regular posts of brands and internet icons

According to data gathered from multiple surveys, Twitter is the one and only SNS where you should publish numerous contents on a daily basis. Unlike IG and FB--its major competitors--Twitter is chronological. Depending on the number of your followers, the Tweets on your home page may have short lifespans. Hence, you need to publish regularly.

Digital marketers must take advantage of this feature when integrating informative or entertaining content.

Such content provides information and keeps the audience engaged and makes your Twitter stay "relevant." This social media allows for the publishing of polls, live streams, texts, video, and images. Such digital contents encourage conversation and lead to conversion in many ways.

- Twitter can effectively showcase the voice of your brand

Having a flexible posting schedule, social media is indeed a social network where you can develop your brand's voice and its public personality. Dependent on the niche, tweets can be sassy or authoritative. For example, fast food chains, like MC Do, have revolutionized their branding strategies with the social network, in a comedic and notable way.

Even Moonpie, a forgotten brand, has been resurrected on the social platform. Now, fast food has a solid following of over 275,000. Many people anticipate Moonpie's humorous and engaging content, regularly. Now, that is Twitter marketing done right!

Twitter also archives your brand voice. However, the open format of the platform can sometimes become problematic, especially when old or problematic posts resurface.

- TweetDeck

TweetDeck allows you to monitor your Twitter account for free. To date, it's considered Twitter's most powerful tool for digital marketing analytics.

If you have a Twitter account, Tweet Deck can prove to be useful for you. It's a free marketing tool for monitoring and identifying hashtags, keywords, and accounts you need to watch and follow. TweetDeck generates feeds for specific parameters.

Being an excellent tool for staying relevant and updated with your most-valued followers and mutuals. With it, you don't need to utilize your main Twitter page when manually searching for keywords. You won't miss important tweets as well.

The application allows you to watch the activities of your competitor and the community, in general. This makes Tweetdeck a very impactful marketing tool for knowing your customer base more. Tweetdeck can also greatly aid in creating a social media marketing strategy since the app provides valuable information about valuable prospects and loyal consumers.

For instance, if a user complains about you using the same keywords as that of your business rivals, you can instead recommend your products\services as a possible solution that could address his/her pain points.

Furthermore, the ability to monitor keywords on the platform, while being updated with the discussions relevant in the industry. With this, your optimized future marketing plan can address the needs of your consumers and industry trends.

For example, Rihanna's business, Fenty Beauty, has been received well for its various make-up shades that are compatible with any skin tone, whether black, beige, or white. By focusing on relevant pain points, like "conventional make-up being non-inclusive to individuals with dark tones," Fenty Beauty, addressed the issue quite well. They researched well and offered products that can really solve the issue.

In chapter? You'll learn how to craft a winning social media strategy that you can use in the major SNS platforms.

☐ On Twitter, influencers can greatly improve the results of your ad campaigns

In 2019, it was revealed that influencer campaigns tweaked for social media marketing yield a return of approximately $7.50 for every dollar spent on them. You can't doubt the power to influence such modern-day social media celebrities.

However, internet icons and seasoned influencers have oversaturated Instagram. This makes influencer campaigns more relevant on other SNS websites.

In particular, Twitter offers a great potential for SMM and B2B marketers. New surveys reveal that purchase intent doubles when leads see Twitter posts from both influencers and brands.

Approximately, 40% of the users on the social media platform say they've bought a product as a direct result of a Tweet from an influencer. In addition to that, 48% of Twitter users say that they greatly rely on the recommendations of social media icons, like influencers and YouTube personalities, when making purchase decisions. These numbers imply that Twitter offers great marketing opportunities.

- Your Twitter profile can improve the traffic on your website or other social media pages

Profiles and pages on social media platforms are like home pages; they can serve as the gateway to your other content and as a table of contents page. Twitter is a good place to get to know your business better and how your consumers view and interacts with your brand.

Did you know that approximately 50% of users that visit a profile on the platform also redirect to the website linked to the profiles? This is especially true when the URL of the site is included in the Twitter bio. In the following sections, you will learn how to write an eye-catching bio and how to optimize your profile for your business.

50% of the time of such visits inspire further research. With that, you must remember Twitter is a good place to showcase and develop your brand's voice. Therefore, a Twitter account providing playful content must not redirect to a very formal website.

The brand voice should remain consistent across all the SNS channels dedicated to your business. Otherwise, consumers and prospects will be confused. They may even leave the Twitter page without being converted to a lead.

- ☐ Advertising expenses can be low, but effective

Paid advertising can go as low as $1 per day. Nevertheless, the real strength of every paid advertisement is optimization. Funneling and Twitter Advertisements can guide you to campaign creation processes. You can also get free insights and parameter suggestions to boost impact.

Next, if the right setting is modified, the social media platform will pace or minimize spending according to the results. This ensures that you aren't spending unnecessarily and that your ad is fulfilling your marketing goals.

In fact, Twitter ad campaigns deliver a 40% higher ROI than other forms of paid advertising. What's more, you greatly customize each ad for your own preferences.

- ☐ Branded hashtags can make community management easy as pie

Hashtags are the king among social media and marketing discovery tools. Not only do they help prospects see you on Twitter, but your post could also appear on Google! If you optimize your tweets properly, that is possible.

In particular, branded hashtags allow your followers to share their own experiences on other social channels, like Facebook and Instagram. Branded hashtags comprise over 70% of Twitter's whole hashtag landscapes.

A branded hashtag boosts your business' uniqueness, even though it could just be a company name, tagline, or the name of a service or product.

How to create an effective one? Please follow the guide in the next section.

How to Gain Thousands of Twitter Followers in 30 Days

Fast and easy to use, Twitter is indeed one of the most effective social media platforms for boosting your brand's audience and for growing your presence in the digital world.

Aside from being user-friendly, Twitter can also upgrade your social media marketing plans to another level. With its social analytics features, you can monitor what's happening on each tweet, for free and on real-time.

Twitter simplifies the idea of "growth" to its simplest form: "The more followers you have, the more impressions you'll get. The more people see and engage with your tweet, the greater your influence will be in your industry.

Now that that secret has been revealed, it's time to talk about the best and the most effective ways to gain Twitter followers. Are you ready? Please go ahead and dive in!

☐ The Tweet Combo!

Sometimes, you can compare tweeting to boxing. Maybe, this sounds absurd to you, but try to picture it this way.

Tweeting with strategy is way too different than just tweeting randomly. It's like punching into the air versus landing a clear punch onto your opponent's chin.

Strategic tweeting, a form content publishing, always follow a marketing plan. It creates opportunities for your account to grow an audience, comprised of people interested in what you offer. Strategic tweeting can generate splendid results, like earning 400 Twitter followers per day.

Tweet combo means tweeting strategically on a regular basis. The more you tweet, the more your audience will start to believe that you exist as part of their world.

People often forget the presence of the users who post seldomly. Also, Twitter will even stop recommending you to your loyal fans if you become inactive in a month. The thing is, the more you tweet regularly, the more your audience remembers you.

Keep in mind that our world is very fast-phased, and people move fast. They often lose focus on things that they don't encounter quite often.

So, if you can create content regularly and tweet more often, you're actually cementing your presence into the minds of your prospects. They will remember you subconsciously.

Now that that is given, you also need to know that *perfect timing* is essential. According to Sysomos, a pioneer of media intelligence and outside insight, the perfect times of tweeting are between 11 a.m. and 3 p.m. EST.

That means morning and mid-noon offer more engagement.

However, tweeting following a goal is an excellent strategy as well. According to Neil Patel, one should aim for at least 1 to 5 tweets per day, in order to maximize engagement.

In addition to this, according to statistics, tweeting on weekdays is more effective than posting on weekends.

☐ Make Your Tweets Visually Edible

Here's the thing, "a good stuff will always be a good stuff." Even if you have thousands of tweets in your profile, but they're not visually edible, you will not garner good results.

What's a visually edible tweet? It's a post on Twitter that is clear and eye-catching.

A visually edible content is content that can be consumed by your audience. Just like food, people only pay and spend money on meals that taste good. And people tend to spend money on those that look good.

If your tweet can't capture the audience's curiosity, it's a waste of effort. You won't get that many likes, and nobody may even "expand" the tweet. Engagements and impressions will be low.

In strategic tweeting, timing and tweeting frequency are not all that matters. If you wish to grow the number of your, you must always consider the following factors:

✓ Why people tend to click on certain content

✓ Why are they attracted to the Tweet, image, or video?

A visually enticing content is a win-win move for every Twitter user. This includes the viewer and the brand owner. If you can play the game of attraction in social media, you've a one-way ticket to success.

How can you join the game? Try to play with colors and learn some editing skills. But, most of all, study trending tweets, in order to get some ideas that you can incorporate into your next post.

Remember, always adapt helpful factors. Those that can boost engagements should not be ignored. For example, use GIFs to boost impact, in seconds.

Also, remember to keep your tweets concise. You can only use 160 characters in each tweet. Attach photos that compliment your tweet. You can also use image quotes to continue the thought of your message.

A straightforward text is easy to consume because it's easy to understand. Images and other medias should be meant to catch attention or affirm a thought. It's as simple as that.

☐ Optimize Your Twitter Profile for New Followers

Up to 15% of the daily promotional tweets on the platform are made by bots. Those who can differentiate a bot tweet from a human-generated post will see bot-using brands as insincere and low-quality.

As a marketer, you must do everything that you can to prove that a human regularly operates your Twitter account.

Aside from having a diversified content strategy, here some subtle steps to make your Twitter profile friendly, valuable, and authentic.

1) Use a clean profile photo

Show them that whoever operates your brand is a real person. As reported by the psychology of social photos, a clear image can serve as a replacement for a high-resolution

What's more, it's a great way to show who you are. However, your photo must exude the same personality you've portrayed in your social media profile.

For example, using a gothic profile photo while featuring cute and feminine images in your tweets would confuse your viewers.

2) Include location details, industry keywords, and relevant tags

With less than 200 characters, you must be able to describe the purpose of your brand, what you do, and give a clear indication of what you constantly offer/feature.

You may also include your title, where you operate, and what companies you work with, but this depends on your brand persona. In the next section, you'll learn how to craft a relatable and inspiring brand persona that could capture the hearts of prospects.

Remember, your brand isn't for boasting, but for propagating your business or online presence as an icon.

For example, if you belong in a fanbase and you regularly tweet about news and fun facts about your idol, then your followers won't care much about your profession.

Tweeting about your corporate career, ranting about your toxic workmate, or sharing issues about your workplace won't look good for your brand. This is especially true if you provide freelancing and professional services.

3) Give them a taste of your personality or professionality

Professionality means the art of maintaining a professional image. When maintaining a brand or running an online brand, that is very important.

4) Use a Lead Magnet to Grow Your Twitter Following

Everybody loves freebies, especially if it's something useful or memorable.

What's a lead magnet? Is it a person? In marketing, a lead magnet is any free service or item given away to select or random individuals who've fulfilled something.

Some examples of lead magnets include:

- ✓ Coupons
- ✓ Free digital content
- ✓ E-Newsletters
- ✓ Free consultations
- ✓ White Papers
- ✓ E-book

- ✓ Samples
- ✓ Trial subscriptions

Lead magnets can help in building authority and trust. It also enables you to show your potential to prospects and you aren't just being too business minded.

At all times, you must show your consumers that you're there to be of service, not just to generate profit.

Further, with a lead magnet, you're proving that you can deliver what you promise, and you have the capability to aid and fulfill what your prospects need.

Share some free resources, like articles, tools, videos, and e-books, and you'll see users following you in no time.

5) Contribute Some Guest Posts

If you have a talent for writing, guest posting on popular publications, like Forbes and Hubspot, and prominent blogs can boost your follower count by 34%.

However, before guest posting, make sure that your Twitter profile is in its best appearance. Avoid off-topic tweets and optimize your bio and pinned tweet. Don't forget about your header and profile picture.

After publishing your content, the traffic to your Twitter profile may considerably increase. So, you must not waste such an opportunity. Your Twitter profile needs to look as eye-catching and engaging as possible.

By guest posting, every article or blog post you publish becomes a beacon for organic web traffic. If the readers like your content, which could be a blog, press release, product review, etc., they will be compelled to know more about you and crave for more from you.

According to SproutSocial, guest posting, coupled with social media marketing, may bear the slowest lead generation rate. However, it can bring in targeted prospects and people who really need something from your brand.

If you combine guest posting with other Twitter lead generation styles, like the ones discussed in the following sections, the number of your followers will steadily grow in the span of 30 days.

6) Increase your CTR to Boost Engagement

CTR stands for Click-Through Rates. Improving your CTR includes increasing the rate of profile clicks, image clicks, and tweet expansion (tweet detail views).

On Twitter, tweets with one or more of the listed characteristics below get more clicks.

- ✓ Posts with appealing images
- ✓ Tweets with popular, trending, or industry-relevant hashtags
- ✓ Links to informative videos and other valuable digital resources
- ✓ Inclusion of one or more lead magnet
- ✓ Link at the beginning or the bottom of the tweet

With all of these, you can improve your tweet's CTR. You can also increase your profile's lead generation rate. Additionally, in some industries, like the gaming industry, memes are very popular.

7) Offer Support and Information and Answer Industry-Related Questions

This is very basic in Twitter marketing. To generate targeted leads, post-industry-specific content. By doing this, you provide valuable content and you're silently making your brand known, as a reliable and noteworthy entity.

However, there's a caveat. Your existing followers must be able to appreciate your tweets. And you must include hashtags relevant to your industry or niche.

You can either search manually or use online tools, like Topsy and Hashtagify. These two let you search for keywords you can use as hashtags. You can also look for trending questions related to your niche, by using such tools.

With the right hashtag, you can also find relevant questions. Once you find users that need help or answers, respond with your own feedback. By doing this, you gain targeted followers who will find value in what you tweet.

They could become silent followers. These are those who will serve as additional statistics for your profile, but they could also be future clients. And then, there those Twitter users who will follow you like a vulture, check out your every tweet, and retweet or send hearts like an avid fan.

You can also provide a support channel for the prospects and customers of your product or service. For example, UPS devices can be tricky to use, and some brands have limited lifespans. That's why many consumers are baffled as to how to use and troubleshoot such devices.

Sony, one of the best electronic hardware providers in the world, came up with a timely response channel on Twitter. By doing this, they've boosted their UPS sales by 64%.

8) Search for Competitor Tweets

This is still related to the tip above. And you may need to use what you've just learned in order to implement this marketing tactic.

In the same way, as you find inquiries on Twitter, you can look for your top competitor's tweets. You can research for this while finding complaints and opportunities to sell.

If you see customers who're unhappy with the service or product of your business rival, you can offer a free consultation or an offer with a freebie. However, don't do this publicly. Contact the prospect publicly, as this is a form of poaching and must not be done out in the open.

In addition, please don't be explicit and avoid mentioning words like "check us out" or "we offer better service than." This can be off-putting to some and could lead to defamation of your brand.

Contact the prospects via email or Twitter direct messaging (DM).

9) Include Share and Twitter Buttons on Your Website and Other Social Channels

If internet surfers like your digital content on your other social media pages, they may follow you on Twitter as well. By providing valuable content in all of your social channels, including Facebook, Instagram, YouTube, and TikTok, you can boost your followings on other platforms. This is why it's very important to only publish enthralling, eye-catching, and valuable content.

Even better, include your Twitter username in your employees' email signatures, in your email templates, and in the newsletters of your other brands.

In addition, consider incorporating Twitter and share buttons on your website. And also, don't forget to place them at the bottom part of your blogs and vlogs. If you're on YouTube or any other video-sharing site and you have more than 1,000 active subscribers, then also include your Twitter handle there.

10) Leverage Twitter's Search Function

Search for people on Twitter; search for prospects and possible followers. Even if some users may not likely buy from you, entice them to follow you as long as they may do.

They may not contribute to your sales, but they could be future likers and will be included in your social media statistics. The more followers you have, the more trustworthy your brand looks to prospects.

Twitter's search tool isn't just for finding hashtags. It's also excellent for looking for people, especially those who could be interested in what you offer. Try visiting a follower who constantly likes your tweets. Then, scroll down his/her timeline (TL).

Between his first few latest tweets, you can see the "Who to Follow" section. Click "Show More" and you'll see a bunch of other people who has the same taste as you follow. All of them are your leads now!

Aside from that, you can also look for your business rivals. Choose one that has many followers. Now, if you check out his followers, you'll see those who could be his "current" most active followers. The users who have liked his most recent tweets can also be considered active. They can be your leads as well.

11) Get Involved in Twitter Chats

Twitter chats are different to direct messages. They're like Facebook group chats, except for the fact that the chats are public. Everyone can see them. Even an unregistered Twitter user could find your chats and mentions on Google and other search engines.

If someone search for your Twitter handles on Google, they can easily find your profile and everything you've tweeted publicly. This also counts your replies to Twitter chats. So, any negativities you've replied to on Twitter will appear as well. And the messages of users and trolls that have said something bad about you can be seen too.

That's why you need to keep your cool, avoid replying negatively to anyone, and stay friendly, cordial, and professional at all times. Online, everything you say will reflect on your brand. With all of these, Twitter chats may seem like something to be avoided.

However, the benefits out weight the disadvantages.

Twitter chats are public conversations that transpire on Twitter at a specific time and date. It's usually about a specific topic, which the chat moderator has chosen. A hashtag is always included.

A hashtag is very necessary, as it allows people to find the chat and follow it. If you don't use the hashtag in your replies, the other participants will not see your tweets.

Hosting a Twitter chat or getting involved in one can help you further establish credibility and authority in your online community. It allows you to connect with like-minded individuals.

Yes, this may take time, but it could result in many new followers who are interested in what you do. Plus, you've already built rapport with them because of the Twitter chat. They won't follow you unless you haven't entertained them, or they've seen you as someone worthwhile and authentic.

That's why when you're engaging in a Twitter chat, please be cordial and friendly as much as possible. When you're chatting with fellow adults, remember that boundaries are healthy and foster respect and a reasonable sense of distance.

By engaging in Twitter chats, you can also offer support and answer inquiries. On top of all that, you can develop meaningful relationships with prospects and followers who may support your channel as long as your active. According to Neil Patel, one of the world's most successful online entrepreneurs, engaging in Twitter chats is probably the best way to grow follower count, without having to follow back.

Creating a Twitter Marketing Plan

Like on other social platforms, marketing success on Twitter requires strategic planning and the will to stand out. Plus, regular activity and hands-on engagement should be prioritized.

You must always approach social media marketing with an action plan, whether you're on Twitter, Facebook, or YouTube. Understanding each SNS platform works is your ultimate key to success.

For Twitter, please follow the step-by-step guide below. The guides for the other social channels are detailed in their respective chapters.

1) *Write down achievable and clear-cut marketing goals* for your campaigns on the platform.

2) *Create an appealing and easy-to-remember Twitter handle and profile name.* Your name and username must also reflect your brand's voice and personality.

3) *Discover what's trendy in your industry* and *take advantage of "trend jacking."* Incorporate this in your marketing plan.

4) *Post consistently* and *schedule Twitter campaigns.* For this, you can use a variety of marketing tools, like Buffer, Hootsuite, Tweetdeck, Socialbakers, etc.

5) *Design pithy and concise tweets.* For longer messages, link your blog post and other social channels.

6) *Always include high-quality visuals* in your tweets. They must make the tweet engaging and memorable. Think if it this way. When your leads remember your brand, the number one thing they should visualize is your memorable tweets and valuable content. Your marketing plan should be based on this goal.

7) *Make the best use of hashtags and keywords.* The best hashtags include keywords. For example, the #CatCare101 has incorporated the keyword "Cat Care."

8) *Include scheduled polls in your marketing plan* and *ask questions from time to time*.

9) Craft a branded hashtag, optimize it, and use it in almost every tweet.

10) If your Twitter account is quite old and you've used it for personal use, it's advised to *rebrand* and *repurpose old tweets*. If your brand has been around for two years on the platform, *leverage your best-performing tweets* by retweeting or posting something similar. Make some minuscule changes in the texts, headers, and images.

11) *The secret to garnering high engagement and amassing loyal followers is "interacting with the tweets of your prospects."* Comment on their tweets, share their content, and respond swiftly if a customer contacts you.

12) *Tweet when your prospects are most active*.

13) Host contests and conduct giveaways that can boost your chances to go viral. These also give you a reason to ask for retweets and mentions. You may also use this strategy when creating a branded hashtag.

14) According to Neil Patel and other well-known digital marketers, avoid content overload and publish three to five times a day. Space your social media posts and avoid tweeting in bulk.

15) Employ Twitter cards so that your posts will be click-enticing. Twitter cards allow you to take advantage of Twitter's extensive social analytics features.

-Twitter Cards have Different Types:

☐ Summary cards

Summary cards contain a header/title, thumbnail, and description. This is perhaps the way to link outside content in your tweets.

For example, digital artists often use pixiv and Twitter side-by-side. When they post something on Pixiv, they use a summary card to link their work on Twitter. You can also see a small preview of the posted image.

- Summary cards type 2

The second type of summary card allows you to feature a prominent image in your account. With this, you can showcase an enticing high-quality image or thumbnail that links back to your outside content.

- App cards

App cards enable you to link a download button to an app or intellectual product, like a song, video, or e-book.

- Player cards

Player cards feature audio, video, and images. Utilize your Twitter account to deliver breaking news and timely content.

Tweet Your Images Properly

If you ask beginner social media marketers "what's the hardest part of Twitter marketing?" they'll answer, "tweeting images." Unlike Instagram, Twitter doesn't offer advanced media editing functions. Yes, you can add emojis and improve some lighting elements, but these are a far cry from IG's built-in editing tools.

Also, using Twitter's editing tools doesn't guarantee that your image will appear rightly. Those who have no knowledge of *the proper ways to tweet images* find their photos misaligned and just outright ridiculous looking.

If you don't follow the tweeting tips below, you may lose your head in the published image or half of it in your next Twitter selfie. Just look at the example above.

- ✓ For profile photos, the recommended size is 400 x 400 pixels. The maximum file size is 2 MB.
- ✓ The aspect ratio for header images should be 3:1.
- ✓ The most recommended image size for tweets is 1500 x px.
- ✓ For in-stream photos, 1600 x 900 pixels is the most optimal size.
- ✓ The recommended aspect ratio for mobile is 16:9 and 1:1 and 2:1 for desktop.
- ✓ You can only use images in GIF, PNG, and JPG formats.

- ✓ With the Twitter app, the maximum upload limit is 5 MB.
- ✓ With a web browser, you can upload GIFs and image files up to 15 MB.
- ✓ For fleets, the pixel size should be no lesser than 1080 x 1920.
- ✓ Fleets are perfect for mobile viewing.

Here are some more recommended sizes for the most used tweet formats on the social platform:

- ☐ For multi-image posts, the minimum required resolution per media file is 600 x 335 pixels. For the most optimal results, use larger files with better resolutions.
- ☐ The maximum file size for website cards is 20 MB. Those that have a 1.91:1 aspect ratio needs to be at least 800 x 418 pixels. If it has a 1:1 aspect ratio, the resolution of the file must be 800 x 800 pixels.
- ☐ 1.91:1 direct message card requires 800 x 418 pixels for best results.
- ☐ Carousels require at least a 1:1 aspect ratio and 800 x 800 pixels. If the file has a 1.91L1 ratio, the resolution must be at least 800 x 418 pixels.
- ☐ The max file size for Twitter cards is 3 MB and the minimum resolution is 800 x 418 pixels.

Tweets with GIFs, images, or videos garner more CTRs, likes, and retweets than text-based tweets. In truth, Twitter posts with high-quality visual content are four times more likely to garner engagement than plain text tweets.

Hence, creating appealing visual content, with the right size, definitely matters. Nobody wants their ads, tweets, and selfies to look distorted and misaligned.

Inorganic Twitter Marketing: Paid Advertising on Twitter

You can also combine organic and paid campaigns. Both organic and inorganic SMM allow you to reach people who are not following you. However, promoted tweets don't rely on user experience since Twitter blends them in timeline feeds. Often, users perceive promoted posts as ordinary tweets, unless they see the difference.

Promoted tweets are labeled. You can see them "promoted" sign on the upper right corner of the post. The majority of Twitter users don't suspect that such posts are "promoted tweets." Twitter blends them well with normal tweets.

On the platform, combining both forms of marketing can bear many fruits for your brand. However, your Twitter account needs to be eligible for the program and must comply with the ads policies. Also, your header and profile photos should be high-quality images, not GIFs.

Lastly, you must include a URL in your bio. Your bio must be able to entice prospects to visit your website and other social channels. Your account should also be public, not suspended or deactivated.

-The Different Types of Twitter Ads

- ☐ Promoted Tweets

These look like ordinary tweets. Nevertheless, you need to pay for them to appear on the home pages of your prospects and followers. This may sound useless, given that Twitter allows for 100% engagement. But, promoted tweets enable you to reach a broader audience.

- ☐ Promoted trends

Promoted trends are like branded hashtags. But they fall under the category of "paid content." These have a high potential to grow viral.

They could be seen by thousands of people, if not millions. Unlike branded hashtags, promoted tags appear on the sidebar of every active prospect on the platform.

- ☐ Automated advertisements

This option allows you to automatically promote your first tweets of the day, for $99.

-Setting Up Your First Ad Campaign

1) Register your existing Twitter account to Twitter ads so that it will be legible for the service.

2) Secondly, set authentic goals for your Twitter advertisement campaign.

Here are some objectives you can use as references:

- ✓ A specific number of tweets follows,
- ✓ Improving engagement figures
- ✓ App downloads and installations
- ✓ Conversions, such as profile clicks, and website clicks
- ✓ Video views, image clicks, and content expansion

3) Thirdly, you must name your ad campaign. In this step, you should also total the expenses, set a daily budget, and specify the schedule of posting.

4) Defining target options is next. When optimizing the campaign, set some demographics, like age, gender, location, and language.

5) Before launching the ad, campaign or publishing any promoted tweet, review everything first. Make sure that you've properly defined all demographics. Try to execute some mock tests using a third-party software.

Your Cheat Sheet to Twitter Ads

Here are the top tips for repurposing top-performing tweets and leveraging Twitter ads campaigns.

- Act quickly. Digital marketing is like stock investing. Opportunities for marketing and monetizing trends don't last long.

- Your followers, fanbases, and prospects won't always be there to watch you online. Right now, grow your following, improve your brand's awareness, and build rapport with as many people as you can.

- Incentivize people and offer limited-time rewards. By doing these, you can urge people to take action, immediately. Add call-to-action in your tweets and use actionable words like "low stock" and "limited slots only"

- Always include a brand introduction in the ad copy section. Make it brief and avoid adding unnecessary jargons. Use your words wisely.

- Create ads and focus its content to the immediate needs of your prospects. Use this technique for your brand's seasonal offers.

- Incorporate efficient call-to-actions. When you're offering sales, emphasize the number of discounts people can get. But avoid mentioning the amount they'll save.

- ☐ Don't forget to offer free stuff like guides, e-books, checklists, tutorials, etc.
- ☐ Leverage Twitter's targeting options. And *always* take advantage of trending hashtags related to your offers.
- ☐ If it's possible, leverage influencers in your niche. Social media users greatly trust internet icons and their recommendations.
- ☐ However, only contact, reward, and work with influencers who are passionate at what they do. Check their sponsored tweets, in order to know the quality of their content.
- ☐ Some influencers post content that sounds too promotional and overly obvious. Avoid them.
- ☐ Take advantage of events, like Father's Day and Mother's Day. Doing so can improve the results of your Twitter ad campaigns.
- ☐ Once everything is ready, don't launch the campaign yet. Test its efficacy and review the results using social media analytics.

How to Track Campaigns on Twitter

For analyzing the results of Twitter campaigns, various SMM analytics tools are available on the Web. But you can opt to use Twitter's free analytics tools.

For some well-known marketers, including Neil Patel and Dan Lok, Twitter Analytics is their go-to tool when checking out ad or tweet insights and account performance.

Twitter Analytics doesn't require you to install anything. You can also check the statistics on your smartphone. By clicking the bar icon next to the heart button, you can see the performance of the tweet in real-time.

You can also go to www.analytics.twitter.com. It's also accessible in the Profile Menu. Click the More option and open the Analytics section.

In the Account Home, you can collect data about your top-performing tweets. You can see the number of profiles visits each tweet has generated. The statistics also present the number of impressions and the total engagements of the post in question.

In the Videos section, you can check out and monitor in real-time the performance of all your videos. This includes statistics for video views and completion rates.

The Conversion Tracking section provides insights about how well your tweets are generating leads, followers, and customers. Although they aren't virtually located on Twitter, you can also collect data relating to your mobile app events and your website.

This section is very important, as it can greatly help in crafting your brand's voice and social media persona. It generates sample prospects according to the clicks, behavior, and search history of your profile visitors.

Accordingly, you can use the data you've gathered to optimize and leverage your future tweets. Doing this can result in higher conversions. To use this feature, you must own a website, with a registered domain. You must also include a site tag and install Twitter's tag on your website.

Further, you can make use of Twitter ads and cards to collect more insights and analytics. These can greatly help in defining target audiences and knowing more about their likes, tendencies, and online behavior. By doing this, you can craft a more accurate social media persona, which you can incorporate to your Twitter marketing strategy.

Aside from Twitter Analytics, there are also third-party tools that you may find useful whenever you're monitoring campaign results. Some of them are Buffer, SproutSocial, Tweepsmap, Twitonomy, and Brandwatch Consumer Research. Although most of them require paid membership, some offer free analytics tools.

-How Do Twitter Algorithms Work?

Twitter's algorithms, like IG and FB's algorithms, are all about engagement and personalization. All social media algorithms are powered by machine learning. With this, they can sort content and follow ranking signals. Twitter's ranking signals include relevance, recency, engagement and rich media.

- Recency

This relates to how recent a post was published.

- Engagement

Engagement refers to the collective engagement of users to the tweet. This includes likes, retweets, and comments.

- Rich media

As mentioned earlier, tweets with eye-catching media get more engagement than plain text posts. Rich media includes GIFs, images, and videos.

- Activity

Activity relates to the actions you do on the platform. The system also considers the type of tweets and contents you interact with. The more active you are, the more Twitter will recommend your tweets to users. The more people you engage with, the more users that will see your most recent posts.

CHAPTER 4: YOUTUBE FOR MARKETING AND AS A PASSIVE INCOME GENERATOR

With the ever-growing popularity of videos on the internet, you can say that you've come to the era where video contents are overtaking images and written text. According to HubSpot, approximately 90% of marketers claim that video content has a higher efficiency rate in terms of conversion.

The result isn't surprising because videos are indeed more engaging. Videos attract more people and drives more traffic. Whether you're an entrepreneur or a budding marketer, you'll want your content to be successful and rewarding.

YouTube (YT) is the number one video-sharing site on the web. It's also now being considered as the top social media, beating Facebook.

The Powerful Statistics

- 74% of adults in the USA use YouTube.
- This social network and video-sharing platform records over 2 billion monthly active users.
- 77% of millennials in the US are active on YouTube.

- Approximately 90% of OTT watchers in North America watch videos on the platform every day.
- 16% of its site traffic are from American users. Japanese people account for 4.8% of its overall traffic. In the 3rd slot are Indian citizens.
- According to Oberlo, Statistica, and Sprout Social, YT is the second-most visited site on the web.
- Users watch more than 1 billion hours of videos on YouTube.
- On average, users and visitors check 8.9 pages on the platform per day.
- In Q3 2020, daily YT livestreams increased by 45%.
- 51% of B2B marketers and decision makers utilize the platform for research purposes. This includes product review videos.
- 70% of users have bought a product online, after watching a video about it on YouTube.
- In the USA alone, this social media giant has made over $5 million in advertising revenue in 2020.
- The number of YouTubers earning $10,000 annually increased by 50%, every year.

All of those are the power of YouTube, and you can harness that power with social media marketing (SMM).

Going Viral on YouTube

If you want your video to go viral, you should consider these helpful tips and make a viral video in no time.

- Elicit Emotion

Emotion drives most people. Considering that statement, you need to visualize a flashback, and let's try to recall those viral videos you have seen in the past. Those videos that have been shared with you by your friends or most likely encountered inevitably because the video is almost everywhere.

Those videos could be hilarious, educational, awesome, extremely gross, sad, etc. What's common in those videos? All of those videos evoke emotions.

GotStyle's 2021 video is one such video. It was hilarious, to say the least. The dialogue and theme of the short advertisement was incredibly charming. The original video garnered over 300,000 views on YouTube.

Our brain connects to what we see, and every visual element could evoke a certain feeling. The visual element that could cause such a change could be a color, pattern of movement, or message tone in the video. Settings and material things can also trigger your brain to create visual interpretations. This interpretation can then give rise to a certain feeling.

For example, red is a dominant color. When used properly, it could convey love, anger, or romance. The color grey, on the one hand, can evoke grief, dread, and sadness. Other dark colors, like violet and extreme shades of blue, can have similar effects.

Combining two elements like color and movements or any combination that conveys the same feeling will surely trigger the audience's emotions.

- ☐ Take advantage of what is trending

By taking advantage of what is trending in your niche, you can make your video go viral. And this can bring in many new subscribers. For example, the Coffeehouse Crime channel was launched in January

2021. At first, it only had less than 5,000 subscribers, and the channel's videos just garnered 3,000 views on average.

As the months passed, Coffeehouse Crime grew, but it was still a far cry from platinum content providers. In April, the channel's creator published a video about the Kyoto Animation's arson case, which was a hot topic that time among anime and true crime enthusiasts. The said video received a lot of positive praise and garnered over 2.5 million views.

The creator had delivered the topic well, and he was able to truly entice many viewers. You can take advantage of any trending subject. This could be an event, news, meme, or person. Using the current trending topic or subject in your niche could improve your video's exposure and engagement, greatly.

For example, if you're creating an instructional video, you can take advantage of a DIY trend. Leverage this as a tool to attract the attention of many prospects. Use it as the theme of your video. Make sure to use the hashtag associated with the trend.

Ask yourself, "What's trending right now in my niche?"

Remember, every trending topic and subject has its category. You should pick what's best suits your brand and video content. And also, take note that a trending topic or subject will only last for a limited time, so you have to act fast before it loses its popularity.

- ☐ Hit their curiosity

Strike where it hurts most! Humans are born curious. You consume things that feed your curiosity. If you can satisfy the audience's curiosity, that could make your video go viral.

If that happens, you can get closer to your marketing goals. However, for you to use this strategy, you need to gain knowledge of the subject matter. As much as you can, know many aspects of the topic at hand. In doing so, you can know more about the pain points and preferences of the people who will watch your video.

You must perform extensive research, in order to take advantage of this powerful trick. For it to work, you must incorporate it right in your future video. And, that segment that is meant to entice your viewers must not overshadow the main subject of your content.

- ☐ Create an attention magnet title or thumbnail

If you're the typical person who consumes YT videos on a daily basis, you may have already encountered videos with an enticing title.

It may have made you click on it. Thanks to its curiosity-triggering title and eye-catching thumbnail, you've finished watching its contents till the end.

Titles and thumbnails could portray your entire video content. Both simply serve as the window to what your post offers. With that, audiences could get a clue of what's inside your video. They could get the gist of the whole story. However, these will depend on the context of both the video and thumbnail.

For example, you could use a popular entity on the internet as an element to your thumbnail, in order to garner more attention. You could also play with words to make your title more powerful and effective.

Many YouTubers abuse this strategy. Instead of providing wholesome and authentic titles, they mislead viewers with clickbaits. Here are some sample clickbaits:

Clickbaits mislead viewers. And, people dislike this marketing style, whether for video titles or news headlines. Yes, this can greatly grow the number of your viewers, but it will ruin your online reputation. What you need to do is to put on honest effort into your videos. Big goals always require great effort.

Nevertheless, keep in mind that you could always equip yourself with the perfect knowledge that can help you achieve success in what you do. In the end, creating a video is fun, so remember to have fun while aiming for the best.

The challenge is there and will always be there. Remember, you could put a massive effort into a single video content but fail to touch the hearts of your prospects. How can you entice them if they can't even see your content? You need thousands of followers if you wish to have many viewers.

How to Gain YouTube Subscribers Fast

Every 60 minutes, 500 hours of YouTube videos are uploaded. That's a lot of competition. With this undeniable fact, you may have lost the will to become a YouTuber. Whether you want to make being a YouTuber your primary livelihood or as a passive income generator, YouTube is an indispensable marketing tool in the digital world. If you're managing a brand or operating an online business, you need YouTube in your marketing plans.

- ☐ Only create YouTube videos that are highly watchable
- ☐ Create a Power Playlist
- ☐ Publish 10- to 15-minute videos
- ☐ Create a branding watermark
- ☐ Publish high-quality videos with good audio and non-grainy visuals
- ☐ Promote your other content in your end screen.
- ☐ Don't focus on quantity, but regularly publish quality videos
- ☐ Write a relevant, compelling, and comprehensive channel description
- ☐ Respond to every inquiry and comment

- ☐   Funnel your viewers to subscriber magnets
- ☐   Make a killer channel tagline and choose an entertaining channel trailer
- ☐   Include a subscribe link in your banner
- ☐   End your videos with a strong call-to-action
- ☐   Promote your channels in e-books and webinars
- ☐   Use a common theme in your channels so that you'll attract the right people
- ☐   Use hashtags and keywords in video descriptions

Why is YouTube Considered the Leader in social media?

YouTube simplifies the formula of social media platforms. It leads the world of digital sharing. It entertains many people from all walks of life. In fact, in 2020, YouTube was the 2nd-most visited site on the web.

Indeed, the power of YouTube in the digital world influences even other social platforms. YT forces them to broaden their capability and include new marketable features. These satisfy users in terms of topic coverage and context.

YouTube is also considered one of the best platforms that offer peer-to-peer communications. This is why it's also considered a social media giant. With its massive userbase and numerous features, it is perhaps one of the best social platforms for share thoughts, ideas, or even promoting one's self-identity.

Whether you're a Vlogger, a content creator, or a business owner, you can take advantage of the wide audience active on the platform.

In addition, YouTube creates opportunities even for common people. It allows anyone to earn money and have a career in the digital world. Even kids can earn thousands of dollars, with YouTube's partnership program.

Unlike other social media platforms, YouTube simplified the idea of how one could earn money. If you become a registered YouTube partner, you can share videos of stuff you love. This could be a short film, a recording of your hobby, or a documentary related to your career. You could also make instructional videos. This is very trendy right now.

The first-ever YouTuber, Jawed Karim, who was also the founder of YouTube, posted an 18-second video featuring himself at a zoo in San Diego. It was just a common video, which featured Karimstanding in front of some elephants, but it garnered thousands of views.

The video of Jawed Karim entitled "Me at The Zoo" is a proof that YouTube is a platform for common people. On YouTube, anyone can share what's happening in his/her life.

YouTube is a people-friendly platform for any race. It has restrictions, of course, but these rules are for keeping the community user-friendly. Like Facebook, YouTube condemns content with racism, sexual abuse, pornography, and violence. Even by saying the word "rape," your video will be demonetized, and your account will be flagged.

Other than those few restrictions, people love YouTube so much because it gives them freedom. They can watch anything they want on the platform.

Not too long ago, many brands and companies produced a short TV video content and air their promotional videos on the platform. Organic videos, even those with promotional content, can be published for free.

YouTube is a free platform, but the marketing power it gives to brands and companies is immeasurable. In addition to this, YouTube allows for the use of hashtags and keywords. These can greatly leverage the discoverability of a video. Google prioritizes video and images with keywords in their filenames. Using hashtags in video description can give your video a high rank on Google's SERP. Often, content from YouTube even rank higher than text-based blogs.

Most successful brands and well-rooted businesses say, "When a brand doesn't have a video on YouTube, its reliability is somewhat questionable."

Today, people don't just rely on written articles and posted images of products. For most product researchers, a video is more reliable than product review articles, which only contain text and images.

YouTube enables people to maximize their learning. With YouTube, one could always reach new audiences, and with Google as the YouTube parent company, every video could be seen in the Google search results list.

Finally, the advantages of using YouTube as a tool for exposure and for transferring information across the internet are promising. Every big name should be on YouTube. If something is not on YouTube, then prospects could question its reliability.

The Do's and Don'ts of Being a YouTuber: Things to Avoid on YouTube

Becoming an earning YouTuber is a bliss. Perhaps, the joy of video sharing is crucial sometimes especially among those people who wanted to be somebody known across the digital world.

Every platform has its own Dos and Don'ts. On YouTube, it's the same. By knowing what to avoid and what you must do is beneficial especially if you aim to be successful in your industry.

YouTube, in its simplest form, also has something to avoid. Here are some Dos and Don'ts of being a YouTuber:

-The Dos

☐ Using of Tags

Using tags is essential if one is aiming for better exposure. Hashtags are important because they improve the discoverability of videos. Proper usage of tags will increase your visibility, not only on YouTube, but also on your other social media accounts. A hashtag regroups related topics together and makes videos easier to find.

☐ Use Thumbnails properly

By choosing the right thumbnail for your video is crucial in YT marketing. This is because thumbnails serve as the window to the content of your video. It can instantly deliver the needed information to your prospect. A good provides a glimpse of what's inside of the box.

In addition to this, many YouTubers are using thumbnails as their clickbait to gain more views. However, a good and well-edited thumbnail is as good as the whole video. If the thumbnail doesn't achieve visual impact, people often ignore the video, and you lose the chance to gain a new view and a possible subscriber.

☐ Self-explanatory Title

Just like thumbnails, the video title holds a quick description of what your video is all about. Give your video a suitable title so that it will deliver a good impression to prospects.

☐ Asking the audience to like and subscribe

Asking your viewers to like your video and to subscribe to your channel whenever is suitable and possible is important. Asking moves people to do things and it also serves as a reminder of what they can do for you. If you built relationships in your community, then many would not hesitate to click that Subscribe button.

☐ Engage your viewers in the comment sections

When content creators reach out to their audience, good feelings are evoked from their audience. Some of them will be able to relate to the video and some will feel special because of the creator's words.

When the creator shows interest to his/her audience in a more personal level, like responding to comments or tagging them to their post, his/her followers will feel more compelled to always engage with him. Their engagements could be likes, views, shares, and comments.

-The Don'ts

☐ Avoid hate words

Trolling elicits attention, in a bad way. Hate words can be intoxicating. And people tend to stay away from negativity. Social trolls can negatively impact your brand if you respond to them.

Once you react to their rude comments, you'll be entering right into their trap. If you engage in a public dialogue that may compel you to say unkind things, you will be ruining your brand's image.

☐ Don't copy other YouTubers too much

For beginners, copying other YouTubers is a good start of how one should create good content for the audience. However, do not copy the style of other people to the point where you can't find what is unique to you.

Every people have their uniqueness that audiences might see interesting. Use your uniqueness and use it as your starting point to create your identity.

What are the Benefits of Live Streaming?

Unlike pre-recorded videos, live streaming lets you watch real-time videos. These are uncut videos that are far from the influence of editing. What streamers say during live streams is often extemporaneous. This is another factor that adds to their charm.

The simplicity of live streaming is also another factor that makes it popular among the members of Generation X, Z, and A. To live steam, all you need is an internet connection, a device for streaming, like a smartphone or tablet, and a streaming platform, such as Twitch, Facebook, or YouTube.

One could always upgrade their live streaming by using some gadgets like high-definition portable camera, which could easily be connected to your PC or smartphone. You could also set up a soundproofing room, with just some cheap carton egg-trays. This can considerably increase the quality of your videos.

However, the accessibility of live streaming is not the main reason why people of today indulge themselves in live streaming. Rather, it's the benefits they could get from it. If one wishes to know what's behind the curtain of live streaming, they will all be revealed in this section.

☐ Growth Possibilities

Social media algorithms greatly favor videos, especially those being live streamed. The growth possibilities in live streaming are very high. Usually, brand owners employ marketing strategies to reach more people and to gain more leads. Most companies use live streaming in forums, webinars, product/service orientations, and many others.

☐ Less Expenditures

With live streaming, you can reduce the overall cost of hosting a survey, live forum, or training program. While increasing brand revenue, it can also reduce expenses.

Traveling, hosting a gathering, meeting, and many other social-related activities cost a lot of money to companies. Perhaps, live streaming requires little knowledge of how to interact with people in front of the camera. Nevertheless, it offers more advantages that can be beneficial for brands, in the world today.

☐ Connections

Live streaming has a growing community that most people today do not know. The live streaming community is mostly comprised of professional streamers, Ninja and PewDiePie. Even the legendary Gordon Ramsay live streams his cooking sessions on YouTube and TikTok. That doesn't include his hilarious raving food reviews.

Live streaming today is a career for many people across the globe. What's more, streamers learn from other content creators and their viewers can learn something positive from them as well.

In real-time videos, everything can happen. According to SproutSocial, 45% of those surveyed who watch live streams say that they prefer authenticity over edited and scripted performances. At times, the quality of the video being streamed is not the reason why people dive into it. Rather, there are those who are just looking for what is true.

The world of live streaming could be risky in some respects. Nevertheless, it has been proven that it can break walls between people and create rapport. Most people today are diving into their devices like they can't live without them. With that, live streaming builds confidence and connects people with each other.

Furthermore, startups and brand owners often take advantage of live streaming. It is advantageous for them because it gives them the power to study their prospects and know their likes and dislikes.

Chapter End

If you're planning to engage in video marketing or any form of digital marketing, YouTube is one of the best platforms for growing a brand or selling a product/service. Top marketers say, "If a brand is not on YouTube, then its reliability is questionable." Plus, YouTube offers a plethora of marketing opportunities.

YouTube is the second most visited website on the web, next to Google. With its 2 billion user bases, it virtually has no competitors. Yes, Twitch and TikTok are emerging video-sharing sites, but they're still far from what YouTube offers to both marketers and casual users.

CHAPTER 5: INSTAGRAM FOR MARKETING PEOPLE AND BUSINESSES

Instagram, the sister company of Facebook, is the 2nd largest social media platform in terms of daily users. It has 500 million active users. Every day, they generate a myriad of likes, views, shares, and comments. In October 2020, 1.16 billion users were active on the platform.

This is no wonder why brands and businesses in Canada and the United States spend over a billion dollars on SMM and influencer marketing every year! Mind you, they only expend that amount on Insta! It has also been estimated that the platform has brought in 20 billion dollars in advertisement spending in 2019. This is according to Bloomberg.

Super Viral, a UK-based service platform, insists that Instagram is a crucial element to any SMM strategy. This Facebook-owned social networking service ranks 2nd as the most downloaded freeware in the Apple App Store. Also, by the end of 2020, "Instagram" was the 10th most searched keyword on Google--the search engine giant.

In 2020, its active user base has grown by 20%. It seems that the platform's growth won't halt anytime soon. Instagram is undeniably a great place in the virtual world to market any brand or business.

Knowing the Facts

Since Instagram's launch in 2010, it has taken over the world by storm. Every year, its massive user base continues to grow. In America, it may seem that everyone, including their cat, is on the platform. Are you skeptical about his? If you are, the facts below can convince you.

- Instagram has more than 1 billion active monthly users.
- About 90% of IG users follow one or more businesses.
- Approximately 80% of users have discovered a service or product on the platform.
- Over 500 million daily stories are registered on IG.
- In the US, almost 130 million people are active every day.
- Next to Facebook, Instagram is the 2nd most used social network.
- IG users browse for an average of 50 minutes per day.
- Approximately 25 million business profiles are on the platform.
- 60% of this social media's active users visit daily.
- 21% check their account at least three times a week.
- 80% of its users have purchased the app.

All of these facts prove that IG isn't just for personal use. With the growing number of influencers and brands on this social channel, what's keeping you from joining them? Perhaps, you have no experience with Instagram marketing yet, and this is what's making you queasy and overwhelmed.

This chapter "Instagram for Marketing People and Businesses" will introduce you to IG marketing and help you delve into its intricacies. From setting up your first business account to tracking your success on this social channel, you can learn all that and more in this easy-to-understand ultimate guide to IG marketing.

The Story Behind the Web's Selfie Capital and Its Significance to the Marketing World

Instagram, which is commonly referred to as IG or Insta, is an American video and photo-sharing social network. In terms of the amount of video published on the platform daily, it can be compared to YouTube. Like Twitter and Facebook, it's also considered a social media platform.

Created and launched by Mike Krieger, Insta was acquired by Facebook at the end of Q3 2012. Available for mobile and web users, this service enables you to upload digital media in seconds. IG's most notable is its high-quality and visually delectable filters. These filters allow you to upgrade dull images to vibrant photos. Plus, when you use IG's filters, you're also improving your post's discoverability.

Regarding the publishing of content, you can choose to share your posts publicly or privately. Being another great tool for social analytics and keyword research, IG enables users to search for public profiles using names and hashtags. Like on Twitter, you can also look for content using hashtags. But there's one catch. On Insta, you can search by location and further customize the results of your searches.

By viewing trending content, you can further improve your marketing research and their results. By liking photos and other forms of media, you can add the content in your field and make the IG algorithms recognize you as an active user.

Furthermore, the most important feature of Insta is its capability to protect your digital media from reprints and republishing. Instagram is known for its high-quality uploads. Despite this, other users won't be able to save your images or videos in its original quality and resolution.

That's the reason why many freelancers, specifically artists and videographers, choose Insta as their main medium to showcase their works to the world. Over the years, millions have become loyal IG users.

Today, members of Gen Z and Gen Y prefer Instagram over Facebook. They account for 70% of the entire user base of the platform.

You can't post anything on the SNS without using your phone. Yes, you can browse, but publishing any form of digital content requires the use of an Android mobile device or an Apple smartphone.

Apple users and other members of groups who earn five to six figures every month, prefer Instagram for their personal and business needs online, as much as Twitter. In fact, Insta beats Twitter when it comes to daily active users.

In its early years, Ig was distinguished by its image uploading function that allows (1:1) aspect ratio with 600 plus pixels, matching the default display width of iPhone 5—the most popular Apple device of that time.

Over time, the SNS added incorporated messaging measures. This, coupled with its growing user base, has made the platform a hotspot for influencer marketing and other forms of digital marketing. In 2015, the aspect ratio was increased to 1080 pixels. The resolution of HD images.

In that same year, the "Stories" feature was also added. This has allowed users to publish videos and photos to a sequential feed. Each post the only accessible for 24 hours. After that, the content is gone forever.

Today, many social media platforms have this feature. This includes FB, Twitter, and YouTube. Checking Stories is a great way to know who among your followers and friends are online.

Launched in October 2010 as an iOS app, it overwhelmingly gained popularity. By January 2011, Instagram already had over one million registered users. Its popularity further exploded after the release of its first Android version, Instagram 1.0. In 2012, it has recorded 10 million users. By Q2 2018, there were already 1 billion users on the platform.

Above all these amazing feats and facts, Instagram is one of the best platforms for reaching Millennials and Gen Zs--the general workforce in this modern-day and the years to come.

The interface and the platform, as a whole is appealing to young adults and today's middle-aged workforce. According to SproutSocial, 18 to 29 years old people comprise the entire user base of Instagram. But the most important statistic of all is the fact that nearly 2 out of 3 American adults in the aforementioned age group utilize the service.

What's more, this SNS service has accounted for a large percentage of Facebook's ad revenue. What do all these mean to you? The answer to this question lies on the list in the next section.

The Pros and Cons of Instagram Marketing

Like other SNS platforms, Instagram isn't a perfect medium. For most businesses that rely on an online presence, IG is the right place for attracting customers, followers, and prospects. But for some, it lacks the necessary features that other social media offers, like 100% engagement and website publishing.

For some types of brands, like those belonging to the B2C industry, YouTube, Facebook, and Twitter are more preferable. [Will cite this fact] On the contrary, Insta is a natural place for attracting prospects and other like-minded individuals. And it's probably the best social networking service for artists, fashion enthusiasts, and photographers.

In this section, you can learn the many pros and cons of branding and marketing on Insta. You can learn whether or not you should proceed or choose other social media platforms for your online endeavors.

Now, what are the pros and cons of IG for business?

-The Advantages

- Gives prospects high-quality visual references of your services and offers
- Sharing brand message is easy and seamless on IG
- Competition on Insta is milder than on other platforms even though having many active prospects
- Unique ad formats
- Instagram has been growing competitively and its user base keeps on growing
- The number of users belonging to Generation Y is steadily increasing
- Hashtagging allows marketers to easily reach their audience
- The availability of easy location tagging
- Responses are registered in real-time

-The Disadvantages

- Specifically created for mobile users
- Time-consuming and not a good platform for text-heavy content

- It isn't an eCommerce-friendly platform
- Images can only be uploaded through a smartphone or by using a PC Android emulator like BlueStacks or KOplayer
- IG is a great platform for publishing images and videos, but it doesn't have room for other forms of digital media, like formatted texts and document files
- Using links and redirecting prospects to other sites can be difficult
- It isn't allowed to use clickable URLs

Making Money on Insta!

Some celebrities and even normal citizens who have many followers are paid tens of thousands of dollars for a single post on Insta. For many, this is their secret ingredient to social media marketing. It may cost marketers some products or money, but having their brand exposed to a myriad of people could mean great success for their business, so any compensation would be met by huge profits.

Many people make big money on Insta, through many ways, not just influencer marketing or affiliate marketing, wherein you have to promote a brand, product, or service on Insta and get a commission for every sale generated by your public post. Earnings depend on your activity, several following, engagement, industry, and ways of getting revenue, which includes the following:

- Promotion of affiliate links
- Sell/market physical and digital products, including e-books, artworks, and high-quality
- Publish sponsored posts
- Create appealing visual content

- ☐ Be a brand ambassador
- ☐ Provide marketing services
- ☐ Write business captions and offer them to brands
- ☐ Create brand logos and headers for sale
- ☐ Look and work under freelancing clients
- ☐ Open your own online store
- ☐ Be an influencer

Outsmarting the Instagram Algorithm

The word could "algorithm" may freak your out since it's often linked to analytics, programming, and other technical science fields. If this is how you view it, you're not wrong. However, you're not entirely right either.

Algorithms do involve codes and machine learning. Nevertheless, you can outsmart the system and their search crawlers, with just simple marketing tips and tricks, like the ones listed in this section.

According to Instagram, six prime factors govern their algorithms: usage, following, frequency, timeliness, relationship, and interest.

- ☐ Interest

Your home feed on Instagram is based on the profiles and pages you follow and the type of posts you've liked and commented on historically. The same can be said with other users.

This algorithm is quite similar to Twitter's algorithm. The more you like a specific type of content, the more posts related to that niche will appear on your feed. For your post to garner high engagement, you need many likers and followers so that your subsequent posts will get many likes and comments.

Technically, what appears on a feed is the combination of the user's behavior on the platform, including the following:

- ✓ Viewed profiles
- ✓ The content of posts frequently commented on
- ✓ Liked posts and followed pages
- ✓ Frequency of Instagram visits
- ✓ Tagged posts

All of that send positive signals to the platform's ranking system. That's why you also need to encourage followers and prospects to visit your profile, comment on your post, and share your content. This naturally drives engagement and makes your content appear on many people's home feeds.

The more users engage with your post, the more impressions it will get. But what's the most important form of engagement on IG? The algorithm values the views, likes, comments, and reshares.

☐ Relationships

Like Facebook, the algorithm prioritizes posts from your family, friends, and profiles you care about. This is why your loyal followers will often the first ones to see and react to your most recent posts. They include the users who always like and "engage" with your content.

The algorithm and the system utilize interactions to serve results in home feeds. In addition, Thomas Dimson, one of Instagram's software engineers, shared that the platform considers the following "activities" when ranking content:

- ✓ Users similar to one's IG name
- ✓ Brand's related to one's interest

- ✓ Users receiving DMs
- ✓ Keywords used related to the given brand
- ✓ Search phrases used by the user

Insta calculates the connection between the user and the factor and the interest level for the profile's posts/contents.

- ☐ Timeliness

Like Twitter, Instagram prioritizes the most recent posts. It always serves the latest relevant content to users. Like you, Insta wishes to please your prospects and followers.

This factor also underscores the frequency and time of your posts. To get these right, you need to consider your audience. You'll hardly get any impression if you post during their work hours or bedtime.

For example, working-class people visit their social media early in the morning, before bed, and during lunch breaks and train rides. You must also consider your time zone. It could be nighttime at your place while it's mid-day in the location of your prospects.

- ☐ Frequency

How often do you post and use the app? If you don't provide valuable content on a regular basis, the system will forget about you and your followers. When this happens, IG will stop suggesting you to many users.

Instagram queue content chronologically. If you publish posts once a month, the chances are that you'll just be suggested to a few new users. And this is only possible if you have a huge following.

- ☐ Embrace IG's latest features

From newly added emojis to the latest editing function, Instagram prioritizes content that has utilized their new offers. The same goes for promoted content and paid advertising.

- ☐ Optimizing and scheduling your stories

IG Stories appear at the topmost part of feeds. The profiles and content that appear there are from accounts that the user in question has engaged with. Like in home pages, past interactions are the determining factors.

But, unlike with feeds, Stories offer better engagement opportunities. That's why many marketers take advantage of this feature. Use it to leverage your marketing campaign. Publish actionable and timely news, memes, HD images, and video clips that can really drive CTRs and profile visits.

In social media marketing, you must treat each option as an opportunity to better improve the results of your campaigns. Use each feature of Instagram to attract and capture the hearts of followers and prospects alike.

By publishing stories regularly, you increase your chances of reaching new viewers. The more views and clicks your content gain, the higher your ranking will be on the social network.

If you're busy, you can use IG Stories with Later. With this, you can schedule future Stories at a specific date and time. You have the ability to stay relevant and engage your existing followers even while you're away.

Furthermore, you can use IG's Storyboard features. You can publish consecutive digital content in the form of a story arc or comic strips. You'll get notifications when your pre-planned captions, links, or images are about to be published.

IG's Stories section is equivalent to Twitter's Fleets.

Top Tips for Using Instagram Reels and IGTV

Instagram's basic ranking factors also apply to IGTV videos and Reels. Beyond the home page, IG serves suggested and promoted

Reels and videos. With machine learning, Instagram bots will serve you content that you may like.

To optimize your digital content for IGTV and Reels, share them with your timeline. A 1-minute or lesser preview will suffice, but make sure you highlight the most enticing parts. And include a short caption that can make you connect with prospects. Don't forget the relevant hashtags!

- [ ] Use emojis and stickers that can generate leads

IG offers many, many stickers. The best ones for marketing are the question stickers, pull funny faces, and emoji sliders. [Insert statistics here] They offer easy and quick engagement for IG Stories publishing. When you're holding a contest or giveaway, be sure to incorporate these.

- [ ] Cross-promote your IG content

Cross-promotion is using all IG's publishing channels for one content. You can make slight modifications, but the publishing time and date for all media need to be simultaneous. With Instagram's growth, many channels have become available such as Reels, IGTV, and Stories.

With these new publishing mediums, you can further improve your brand's conversion rate and guide viewers to your most recent content. For example, sharing an attractive preview or thumbnail of your IGTV video to your timeline. You can also add convert a feed post into a story with an enticing "Tap Here" visual.

Eight Things You Must Avoid on Instagram as a Marketer

Many strategies can help you to perform well on the platform. However, there are also words and activities you must avoid.

Knowing what not to do aids in creating better content and building a better community. After researching your audience and prospective clients, you will have a general idea about their culture, their mannerisms, the values they uphold, and the things/words they deem as undesirable.

☐ Your name and username are the same

Your Instagram username should be different from your profile name. On Instagram, users who use the same name and username are seen as "amateurs" and "beginners." IG usernames are strings of words in lowercase. There are no space or unnatural symbols. Even hyphens aren't allowed; only periods and underscores can be used.

The profile name, however, must be in sentence format and include spacing and capital letters. You can also insert emojis into your profile name. In case you want to use your actual name, which will serve as your brand name, use your first name, middle initial, and surname. You can opt to include or not include your middle initial.

Some celebrities and political figures just use your first and last name. For example, President Barack Obama's Instagram username is @barackobama. Authors and artists may just use their pen name or initials, as in the case of J.K. Rowling.

☐ Opting for an irrelevant Instagram handle

On Twitter, your Twitter handle is your username, which is preceded by the "@" symbol when you're actually on the platform. This is also what your followers and other users utilize to tag you or mention you within the platform. As well, your social media handle is also what search engines use when ranking your profile and posts

In the world of social networks, all of your posts and comments are linked to your profile handle. If your account is public, which is a necessity for Instagram business accounts, your username must reflect your brand, or who you are.

Random names will make it hard for your audience to determine what your profile is all about. Even gamers are specific in choosing their usernames on the platform. For example, DOTA 2 players include the game name "DOTA" in their IG handles. This also remains true on other social channels, especially on YouTube, Twitch, and Twitter.

By doing so, their viewers can immediately know what they're offering. A random name not related to your niche or industry will make your profile look skeptical. Others may see it as a fake profile or dummy account. According to Sprout Social, the majority of users avoid interacting with fake accounts. Furthermore, a random username will be hard for your customers to find you on social.

So, what should be the characteristics of your IG username? It must be recognizable and shareable. Just imagine if your IG handle is @KillerCloudNineCat and your profile is about "taking care of pets." Do you think your prospects will share your content? You may hardly get any likes or follows. If you do garner some, you're attracting the wrong crowd.

☐ Not including an Instagram bio

On Insta, you can only insert your tagline in your profile bio. Bios and taglines are very important in internet and social media marketing. Leaving this part blank is like introducing yourself to someone and saying nothing but your name.

Your bio will depend on the nature of your brand or business. If it's something personal and you're marketing yourself, you can include your hobbies and some emojis and fun symbols. But if it's for professional work, avoid making your bio sound personal. Instead, it must give a brief summary of your skills, your work experiences, and the services/products you're offering.

- ☐ Not using IG stories

If there's something that offers 100% engagement on IG aside from their paid and VIP features, that's IG stories! Every day, over 500 million users use this feature. By using Instagram Stories, you can increase your content's engagement and improve your brand's reach. How is this possible in this platform very similar to Facebook?

You see, all of your online followers can view your IG stories for 24 hours. Why ignore this great opportunity to connect with people. This is the reason why you must take advantage of this free and absolute feature of Instagram. Incorporate it into your marketing plan today, because it may not remain free forever.

- ☐ Not including captions in your posts

At its core, IG is a visual platform for social networking. It's developed for sharing high-quality videos and photos, both in stories and feeds. That's why walls of texts and text-heavy content aren't suitable on the platform. Nevertheless, even though images can conjure a thousand words, the inclusion of a short caption can drive more engagement with followers and their followers.

According to a 2019 survey conducted by Statistica, a video or photo on Instagram without a caption have a lower engagement rate. Plus, the caption allows you to entice your audience to do something, such as clicking the like or share button.

A caption section is also a place where you can insert questions, add a zest to the image, or offer a call-to-action. You may also provide a very short description of the background of the post. These small offerings are critical to driving conversations and building relationships on Insta.

- ☐ Hashjacking

Let this be a rule of thumb in your social media marketing endeavors: Only incorporate hashtags relevant to your post and brand. As mentioned earlier, you can take advantage of trending hashtags to leverage your brand's reach and exposure. However, this is only applicable if it's related to your business.

Suddenly talking about and using a hashtag that is a far cry to your usual content would leave a bad taste to your followers and the people who'll see your post. For example, you constantly provide information about lifestyle and fashion, and then, you suddenly rant about your country's politics using the hashtag "#OUSTthePresidentNow."

What will your audience and followers feel about that kind of post? Hashjacking is frowned upon in the social media world. At best, irrelevant content that appears in trending hashtags is ignored. If you aim to increase your number of followers, the viewers from the trending tag will either ignore your post or report it as spam.

The last thing that you want as a brand manager is to have your account suspended. Plus, your loyal followers may unfollow you if you constantly publish irrelevant content. They followed you for your valuable posts, not to see daily irrelevant rants from you.

If you wish to express yourself, you can. You must create another IG account for that. But be careful of the digital crumbs you left behind. There are some exceptions, though.

During national and international holidays, many hashtags related to the commemoration will trend on Twitter, YouTube, TikTok, and Instagram. It's advised to take advantage of such trends. For example, you can use the hashtag #EarthDay to join events or #MothersDay when you're greeting your own and sending love to all the mothers out there.

Both male and female IG users will appreciate your post, depending on your message's degree of sincerity. That's why, at all times, always offer and provide sincere messages. Use your brand's voice and tone to connect with your audience, whether you're addressing your followers or non-followers.

When your post can capture hearts, then you'll see many new followers on your Insta account.

- ☐ Tagging IG users not included in the photo

You can tag your avid followers who really like most of your content, only if they have approved it or have requested it. Still, be careful of such requests. Some users may just use you to gain traction for their own brand. Building relationships in the online world is great, but you must establish boundaries.

Only do that if you really feel compelled to help the other person. For example, your long-time follower lost her Insta account, or it got hacked. You should help her by sharing her story on your own timeline. Many will gain the sympathy of her misfortune and it will be another plus point for your own brand.

Many people, especially the beginners, tend to abuse IG's tagging function. They'll post photos and tag tens of people in an effort to increase impressions. If you become too persistent, someone you've tag may call you out. This could ignite a public argument, which is something you must avoid.

You must use this feature sparingly. What you must do is tag brands and accounts of influencers with who you desire to connect. Tagging is a great way to catch the attention of other users on the platform, but it can also annoy people.

Hence, you must respect the boundaries of others and learn to set some for your brand. Like your fellow IG users, you don't want to be tagged with irrelevant or undesirable content. Even internet surfers, who are not registered on the social network, can see posts that tagged you. They may get the wrong impression. The same goes for the users you tag to your IG posts.

☐   Using online automated tools to generate likes and follows

You must avoid this at all costs. Just tag President Barack Obama, but don't do this. Yes, it can give you thousands of engagements in the day, but it can get your account suspended. If this happens, all of your efforts will go to waste.

Automated tools that offer thousands of likes and random comments may also harbor malware. This can collect your personal information, your password, and financial details. Using such tools can put your IG account at risk of getting hacked or suspended.

Setting Up Your Instagram Business Account

A generic and unoptimized Insta account will not attract the right people. IG is a platform intended for trendy and in-the-moment content, and it will remain that way if you keep your profile as standard as it can be.

If not zero, only a small number will be converted by your posts and account. To stay relevant, you must post regularly even, if not daily. To attract prospects, you need to have an Instagram account optimized for your business.

Below is the ultimate guide to IG business account optimization. With it, you can learn how to build and maintain a successful IG account. Even as a beginner, you'll be able to grow the number of your followers, have your profile exposed to the right community, and be able to monetize your online presence.

☐   The Prerequisites

There are two ways to create an account on this platform. You can either use a web browser or register on the application with a mobile phone. Remember, you can view media and posts on the website.

However, you can't upload anything, except for your profile photo, if you're using a web browser.

On any social media platform, it's always best to use high-quality digital media, whether it's an image, GIF, or video, for any occasion. That way, viewers will recognize your brand as a reliable entity. This, in turn, improves your authority online.

Foremost, you need Instagram installed on your phone. And you need a personal computer or a smartphone that can handle resource-heavy editing. Adobe Photoshop is an excellent image editor for beginners. It allows you to modify the resolution and the number of pixels you're working on. For videos, Filmora is lightweight video-editing software, which also enables animation and GIF creation.

If your smartphone cannot handle photo and video editing, then you can use your computer. A PC with at least 4 GB RAM and 2.0 GHz clock speed has the capacity to run digital media editing programs and save them in a high-quality format. When you're done editing, just transfer the photo or video to your phone and upload it on Instagram.

You may also need a text proofreader or grammar checker, like Grammarly and Ginger software. You must always publish high-quality content on social media, and this includes texts and stories. As much as you can, avoid typos and grammar lapses in your content.

☐ Research is needed

Once you have all hardware and software you need, you can proceed to research. What needs to be researched anyways? Like on Twitter, you need the right hashtags, keywords, or search terms for your bio, tagline, and first optimized posts. Without these, you can't leverage your IG account effectively. By this phase, your brand voice, tone, and goals should've been set as well.

☐ Optimization

Optimization covers everything on your TL, or timeline, from your profile picture to your first-ever post. Your profile pic is like your logo. It's the first thing that visitors will see, and it serves as your emblem on Instagram. Whatever you do on the platform, your account name and your profile pic are what other users see.

Your profile picture must leave a lasting impression on your viewers. This is also the reason why it's necessary to maintain your image and avoid changing your profile picture too often. Remember, it's your visual marker. When you change it, your loyal followers may not recognize you. This can lead to a decrease in engagement, and subsequently, lesser revenues.

Also, your logo must visually represent your brand, while being eye-catching and easy to comprehend. A logo or an alluring image will do. Profile pictures on IG are automatically cropped into a small circle. Hence, the corners of your chosen image are left out.

Next up is your bio. 150 characters are only allowed in Instagram bios. It's 90 characters shorter than Twitter bios. So, the key here is conciseness and usage of the right words.

Depending on your field, you can use emojis as well, but keep in mind that not all people will view fun signs in a positive way. In truth, professional business profiles should avoid emojis and symbols not related to their niche or industry.

In writing your Instagram bio, you need to write a concise summary of what your brand is all about. If it's a personal account and you just wish to gain a lot of traction, mention the things you will be offering to a crowd, or you can also give an overview of what you can do. Freelancers do this.

On top of all that, you must not forget to include at least two hashtags or keywords in your profile introduction. Tell your followers and viewers about your services, products, or business. Here, you can also encourage IG users, as well as internet surfers, to fulfill a particular action. This could be redirected to your blog, following you on your other social channels, or clicking the "Follow" button.

If you plan to include a link, use a link shortener, like Tiny URL and HubSpot's URL builder. This makes the URL look presentable and minimizes the number of characters it consumes. You may also use Linkr.ee, Goo.gl, and Bitly. Just search for them on Google or other search engines.

For any future edits, tap on Edit Profile to change your bio, URL, name, photo, or username.

- ☐ Manage Your Account Settings

Your IG account will not be completely optimized unless you modify your settings. To do this, tap on the 3 stacked lines in the upper right corner of your IG profile. A drop-down menu will appear. There, click the Settings option. Doing this will open the rest of the Settings menu.

There, you can change your password, enable notifications, make your account public or private, and check posts you have liked. As a marketer, here are the sections you need to check and modify.

In the Story Settings, you can change who can see your Stories and reply or react to users who have done the same thing. It's recommended to let all of your follower's reply and see your stories. To make this possible, go to the Privacy section and open the Story Controls.

If Twitter has "Verified Accounts," Instagram has "Professional Accounts." This allows users to identify such accounts. The Business Tools feature that is only available to those who have Professional Accounts enables users to easily contact you, even non-followers.

The said feature provides in-depth insights and enables you to launch paid advertisements and publish promoted content. To have a Professional IG account, you need to have an FB business page. In your settings, tap Account and click "Switch to Professional Account to access the additional settings.

Once you have that setup, you can switch to your business profile by logging into FB and allow IG to manage your pages. IF you have multiple Facebook pages, choose the right page related to your Professional Instagram Account. Before you can execute all of that, you need to be an "Admin" of the page you wish to use.

Instagram will import relevant data from your FB business page. You can edit all of these data. Earlier, it was mentioned you can change your privacy settings. You can prevent or enable non-followers to see your posts.

For a business profile, it's best to have a public account. You need prospects to see your posts and be able to follow your account without any hindrances. Make sure that Account Privacy is turned off. By doing this, Ig will automatically make your business profile public.

Once you have that setup, you can switch to your business profile by logging into FB and allow IG to manage your pages. IF you have multiple Facebook pages, choose the right page related to your Professional Instagram Account. Before you can execute all of that, you need to be an "Admin" of the page you wish to use.

Instagram will import relevant data from your FB business page. You can edit all of these data. Earlier, it was mentioned you can change your privacy settings. You can prevent or enable non-followers to see your posts.

For a business profile, it's best to have a public account. You need prospects to see your posts and be able to follow your account without any hindrances. Make sure that Account Privacy is turned off. By doing this, Ig will automatically make your business profile public.

The Settings menu also allows you to hide or show comments with specific phrases or keywords. This can come in handy when you're being attacked by trolls or haters. On any social media platform, having haters or being trolled doesn't mean that you're doing something wrong. Sometimes, these are just individuals who wish to hurt your feelings, as well as the image of your brand.

Avoid responding to them. If you retaliate, you're playing right into their trap. Remember, every word you comment or every reaction you make reflects to your brand. IG has strict policies against hate comments and users who use certain words. There is no need to argue with haters or trolls. Social media platforms have options for reporting, suspending, and blocking such individuals. You need to be professional, even when handling such negative people.

Receiving and responding to comments can be encouraging and exciting. But negative comments may offend some of your audience or breach brand values. To update these, tap Privacy and head to the Comments section in the IG profile's settings menu.

Once you have an Instagram business account, you can add up to five profiles. This can come in handy if you plan to manage two or more brands. With one business account, you can add up to five IG accounts. And you can just switch between them without having to log in and log out.

That feature also enables multiple people to log in into one business account. To add an IG account, tap the Add Account button at the very bottom of the settings menu. Now, enter the password and username of the IG profile. You've just successfully registered a profile to your Instagram business account.

Posting and Using IG's Editing Functions

Have you ever wondered why some images look so good on IG? Probably it has to do with the editing process used. Editing photos can take a few minutes or up to a couple of hours. The duration depends on the program being used and the number of edits needed to be made.

Usually, utilizing editing software for PCs will take more time than with IGs editing tools. IG's built-in editor and filters streamline photo editing. However, if you need to edit a lot of things like changing the background or modifying the overall style and medium of the media, you need a high-end photo editor, like Adobe Illustrator or Photoshop.

Years ago, such programs are only available on personal computers. Today, you can install light versions to your phone. Aside from IG's built-in editing tools, many easy-to-use and instant-edit photo editing apps are on Apple App Store and Google Play Store. Choose an application that has a high rating, and you'll have many editing functions right at your fingertips.

With excellent photo editing, you can turn a simple homemade dish into an appetizing culinary masterpiece. For IG's instant photo editor, here's a short, but comprehensive, guide for its easy usage:

1) Choose a high-quality photo. Avoid images with grainy quality, low resolution, and bad lighting. Its resolution must be no lower than 720 x 1200 pixels. The most optimal size is 1080 pixels wide by 566 pixels to 1350 pixels high. 1080 pixels is the maximum resolution allowed by the platform.

2) Proceed to edit. In this step, you need to select an editor. You can opt for IG's default tool. But you can also use third-party apps, such as Snapseed and PicsArt. For Instagram marketing, the most important settings for consideration are HDR, tonal contrast, exposure, sharpness, and effects.

3) Publishing your content with an edited photo. As mentioned earlier, Insta has been designed for sharing images and videos. Surveys have suggested that plain text content doesn't perform well on the platform. The best combination of content on IG is a short high-quality video with a brief description and a properly colored high-resolution image with a short caption.

Note:

When you upload an edited image to IG, the system will automatically crop the image into a square. To change it back to the original size, tap the icon showing two facing arrows. In this phase, you may opt to use or not use IG filters. Each filter exudes a personality that can change the message of the photo. This is discussed in the preceding sections.

4) Next up is "Lux Adjustment." This function provides needed brightness and auto-corrects exposure. Lux can make images more vibrant and emphasizes minor details. To activate Lux Adjustment, click the wand icon at the top right-hand corner of your smartphone.

5) Applying the final edits, you can improve the color and quality of the media you're uploading with IG's editing tools. You'll find them useful even after tweaking a photo or video using a third-party program. You can even modify the structure of an image and its photo alignment.

How to Promote Your Small Business or Personal Brand on Instagram?

Whether in the real or virtual world, high-quality product photos are essential to shopping. With IG's dedicated virtual platform, you can leverage that power to a whole new level.

According to Statistica, approximately 70% of American consumers agree that visually appealing images influence them toward proceeding with a purchase or not. The majority of Instagrammers are on the platform to look for high-quality photos, not for sale text-based pitches.

Instagram is both a social media platform and a marketplace. It can direct traffic to your website and turn views (impressions) into sales. But how can you do this? The platform is there. It's free to use for anyone. You can post photos right after you register, but can anyone see them?

Even if you have optimized your profile and posted delectable images, you and your brand will be going nowhere unless you start implementing the best practices for Instagram advertising and social media organic marketing.

-Using IG for Business and Marketing

You're aware of the benefits of this social platform for your business. Like TikTok and Twitch, Instagram is fairly new to the social networking world. Despite this, it harbors millions of leads that could prove beneficial to the growth of your brand online.

Without leads, it will be hard for you to promote anything on the world wide web. Even if you upload the most appealing digital media out there you will receive zero traffic when you don't know where to start and all you do is confuse your followers.

One thing that is very important in social media marketing is consistency. The significance of this has been tackled in the previous chapters. Maintaining a consistent brand message across your marketing campaigns and on your entire timeline is important in Instagram as well.

If you constantly provide cooking tips and delectable images of food you have made and then you suddenly talk about your travel days your followers and your viewers, those people who see your post with the hashtag you've incorporated will be confused. That's an undeniable fact, and that remains true across every social platform out there.

Your followers like your account and share your post because, in some way, they feel connected with the things you offer. As a social media marketer, you should prioritize what your viewers need from your brand, not your selfies or what you've done for the day. You should only include personal stuff if your activities correlate with your brand voice and business goals.

Even though it's a necessity to connect with people on a personal level you must maintain a degree of professionalism when you're operating your business on Instagram. Remember, empathy is different from ego-boosting acts. Your personal life could be different from your brand goals. Before you post anything, you need to consider some things:

- ✓ Does your post-offer value?
- ✓ Is it inconsistent with the theme of your profile?
- ✓ Can it engage the right audience?
- ✓ Have you included anything that could upset your followers?
- ✓ Do they need to see that digital media?

Actually, there's nothing wrong if you choose to post your selfie unless someone is stalking you, but ask yourself, "Can that photo positively influence your brand's growth? Will it affirm something?

-Insta Marketing Tips for Increasing Traffic to Your Website

Although Instagram is a fairly new social media platform, it already has over 1 billion users. Millions of those people could be leads for your business.

With IG, you can take images and videos, upload them on the app, and share your posts on other social channels, including Twitter, Tumblr, Facebook, and Twitch. On top of all that, Instagram is an excellent place to direct users to your blog, website, or YouTube channel.

If your viewers like your content, they will not hesitate to visit your other accounts because they know that they will get value from them. With words and the right strategies, you can guide people to other websites and fulfill certain tasks.

Now, without further ado, here are the Instagram marketing tips that can help in increasing web traffic.

- ✓ Create IG stories using product links
- ✓ Build a shoppable Instagram feed
- ✓ Provide Instagram only advertisements and promotions since everybody loves a good sale and a ton of freebies
- ✓ Create partnerships with influencers
- ✓ Always nail your captions and dedicate the message to your audience
- ✓ With words infographics gif and other forms of visuals direct people to your website's link wisely
- ✓ Offer content targeted to a specific group of people
- ✓ Provide concise descriptions and limit text and messages to the bare essentials
- ✓ Maximize every marketing channel and engagement opportunities on the platform
- ✓ Always test your campaigns and plans first before launching them and track results on a daily basis

✓ Simultaneously publish on the different marketing channels on the platform

In the last section of this chapter, you will learn how to track your progress on Instagram using the built-in tools on the platform and some third-party apps.

Sample Marketing Strategy

1) Setting realistic marketing goals for Instagram
2) Determine your target audience on the platform
3) Research keywords conduct a competitive analysis and test mock ad campaigns
4) Modify your editorial calendar
5) Craft your brand voice and social media persona
6) Build a brand on IG, establish your brand voice, and incorporate it in each of your future posts
7) Start growing your Instagram followers and think of the ways and mediums wherein you can improve your exposure
8) Convert prospects into followers and turn followers into customers

Developing and Launching Ads on Instagram

Facebook is a saturated place. In contrast, Instagram is a fairly new social networking site that offers the same marketing benefits as the social media giant. The niches are on Instagram, and thousands, if not millions, of people, can be considered as leads.

Instagram is a platform for telling visa stories through various organic and paid formats. Over the years many marketers and advertising companies have seen this platform building higher ROI done in other social networking websites.

Today there are more or less 500 million active users according to Statista. And its rapid growth is undeniably outstanding. Using Insta's advertising options is quite straightforward. All you need is a complete guide.

However, with the regular modification to Instagram's algorithm and the increasing competition in every industry, it's necessary to employ what works. Instagram Advertisements are paid campaigns on the platform. These ads are targeted, meaning they can deliver your digital content to the right people.

Instagram Ads function like Google Ads. The search bots of the social network scan every user's internet history, as well as his or her past likes, follows, and views. The system also takes into account the keywords and hashtags in the posts that the user in question has liked and his/her most favored words when commenting on Instagram posts, stories, and reels.

Once you're done setting up a business account, you can finally take advantage of their ad's services. With these, you can lunch targeted advertising campaigns on the platform. IG, unlike other social channels, provides various targeting options and many ways to personalize an ad campaign. With a plethora of options, you can definitely choose the best one for your brand and prospects.

Developing, launching, and maintaining an ad campaign may seem difficult for startups and influencers who have no prior experience. But this isn't as hard as you think it is. In fact, creating an ad campaign is as easy as clicking the Promote button on your own YouTube video.

By doing this, the system will pull users automatically. You can share your content to the default people group served by the platform. Or you can customize it further to improve projected results.

Once you have crafted a social media persona, you can easily fill in the necessary fields when customizing your future promoted post or ad campaign. You need to enter some keywords and include the location and age range of your brand's targeted audience.

After that, you must set a budget. It's recommended that you opt for monthly billing or quarterly. With this, you can adjust expenses following the results of your most recent advertisements or mock launches.

In order to track the performance of an ad or promoted post, just click the View Results button located at the bottom left corner of your published ad. You can also tweak pre-existing promoted and its targeted audience section. This can come in handy in case you've made some errors when crafting your social media persona.

As well, you must optimize your Instagram ads, aside from editing and using high-quality media. Like the published content on Twitter, Facebook, and YouTube, proper usage of hashtags, keywords, and search terms are also a necessity to ranking high on Instagram. Don't forget to optimize your images, videos, and captions.

Even if your description is just a 3-sentence paragraph or a 2-sentence caption, you must always include keywords and hashtags. And be sure that your message is concise and easy to understand. Call to action or actionable words are also needed.

You need to use your savings or hard-earned money to launch an ad campaign. So, make sure that they are super clear. Keep your message simple; avoid jargons that your viewers will have difficulty understanding; only include undistracting phrases and words.

Selling on IG: The Basics and Creating Your First Shoppable Feed

Have you seen Celine Dion's funniest video on YouTube? It was hilarious, to say the least. Nevertheless, it has clearly delivered

Instagram's message. In the video, Celine is shopping for her favorite products on Instagram with a sprinkle of humor.

Just recently, Instagram has partnered with Shopify in order to provide a "shopping feature integration" designed for marketers, influencers, and brand managers.

It's a great feature for advertising anything on Instagram and for increasing sales. Celine Dion's video is both valuable and entertaining. It gives viewers a general idea of how to shop on this social networking platform.

This is quite unheard of before. Although you can market products within their digital boundaries, SNS apps and websites don't really function as an eCommerce platform, like eBay and Amazon.

Yes, there are many options for content promotion and ad campaigns but features and options for eCommerce are often limited. With IG's revolutionary shopping feature, marketers can directly sell on the app while showcasing high-quality shots of their products.

IG has already been considered a great driver of store traffic for third-party websites. This additional feature allows Instagram users to buy products, add the items to a cart, and proceed to checkout right on Instagram's platform. You can even direct your followers and viewers through IG stories and post captions.

-Setting Up Your IG Shoppable Feed

1) Go to your Instagram profile.
2) Convert it into a business account.
3) Connect your FB page.
4) Upload a product catalogue.
5) Review your account.

6) Fulfill account review and turn on Shopping.
7) Insert optimize texts and images.

Selling on IG: Story Ads

As mentioned earlier, Instagram Stories offer 100% engagement. Organic promotion is quite successful in this marketing medium. If you employ paid ad campaigns alongside SMO, then it's possible to double the results.

Advertisements in IG stories look immersive, and they can be viewed on full screen. Plus, it will only be served on users that will really take interest in the post. This can undeniably boost impressions and engagements. Hence, it could also help you grow your followers and customers. According to Oberlo, Instagram Ads Stories may beat photo ads by Q4 2020 in terms of growth and results.

Unlike photo ads, IG Stories appear on messaging, home feeds, and user timelines. Although an Ad Story is labeled, many will assume that it's just another story by someone they follow.

You can either use text, video, or image in incorporating actionable messages to your promoted IG story. Still, the best way to engage and attract potential clients is to offer high-quality media that showcases your brand's voice and business goals and. Provide answers or hints in your call-to-actions (CTAs)

In HubSpot's 2017 survey involving approximately 100,000 Instagram users, one of five ad stories on the platform gets a click and generates a direct message.

Instagram stories enable you to connect with your followers on a regular basis, without having to flood their home feeds with your daily posts. However, there's one caveat. Instagram stories are only available on the IG mobile app. Those that browse the platform using a web browser will not see your promoted stories.

So, what's the best marketing strategy on Instagram? Combining paid and organic marketing and making use of all the marketing mediums when delivering a specific message are the best ways to market anything on this social platform.

Chapter End

Like YouTube and Facebook, Instagram offers a plethora of marketing opportunities. Having an advertising audience of over 1.2 billion, IG provides massive reach for brands. In recent years, it has kept on growing, and according to HubSpot analysts, it will continue to grow in the future. Instagram was once just a simple photo-sharing app. Today, it's one of the leading social networking platforms in the world.

CHAPTER 6: TIKTOK MARKETING 101

In 2014, musical.ly was created. The application was intended for sharing music and short videos popular to the members of Generation Z (Gen Z). The app instantly became popular because of its lip-synching features and dance video promotions. For two years, it was among the topmost 100 downloaded apps on the App Store and Google Play, and search posted 13 million videos per day

However, in 2018, musical.ly was no more. Bytedance, a tech firm headquartered in Asia, purchased the successful startup app. It merged with TikTok, and from then on, TikTok's popularity has continued to soar by the year.

At its core, TikTok is a video-sharing site, which is quite similar to YouTube. In its early days, dance and lip-synching videos were the raves on this platform. Later on, as it grew and its user base increased, the number of trends and online activities have become more and more varied. Today, TikTok is one of the biggest video-sharing and social networking platforms on the web.

Offering features that YouTube has removed or deemed unimportant, TikTok continues to grow by the day. You can now share not just dance videos on the platform, but you can also use it for marketing yourself or your brand. From tutorial videos to personal records, TikTok has been a haven for artists, gamers, marketers and freelancers looking for new clients.

In just a short time, this social network has expanded massively. And, it continues to add new functions and intuitive features for its growing user base. Much like YouTube and Twitch, the platform has also served as a search engine for people looking for specific services, information, and, most of all, products.

The growing number of influencers on TikTok has contributed to the increase in marketing opportunities on the platform. Since 2018, TikTok has been housing diverse media, from trending music to viral educational videos.

If you want your content to go viral, TikTok is the best place to start. It's a relatively new platform. That's why there are way fewer restrictions and fewer expenses than other social networking sites. That's just some of TikTok's benefits. Here are some more.

The Statistics

- TikTok has 800 million active users.
- Approximately 70% of users in North America belong to Generation Alpha and Generation Z.
- About 25% are millennials.
- In 2011, more than 10 million millennials joined the platform.
- The top brand categories on TikTok are as follows:

  -Fitness

  -Financial and automotive services

  -Home decor

  -Do-it-yourself (DIY)

  -The sporting and entertainment industry

  -Food and beverage

  -Beauty and Health and Wellness

- Fashion and retail

- One of the funniest sides of TikTok is the hashtag #BeanTikTok.
- According to Oberlo, TikTok is the most downloaded software in the Apple App Store.
- The app is available in more than 150 countries.
- 35% of the social platform's users have participated in a hashtag challenge.
- In 2020, over 15 million educational videos garnered thousands of views on TikTok.
- It guarantees 4 million impressions for brand takeover advertisements.

The Benefits: What the Platform Offers

Before planning an ad campaign on the platform, you must adhere to some unwritten doctrine. If you look at TikTok from the perspective of a marketeer, you'll see that it offers:

- Impressions and engagements from the younger generations are guaranteed.
- You can connect with a targeted niche audience
- You'll have the ability to blend information and entertainment seamlessly
- Organic visibility and marketing through the use of hashtags are enabled.
- TikTok is a fairly new social media, so competition is lesser compared on other social channels.

- Unlike YouTube, TikTok allows its users to post videos in just 5 seconds and offers premium editing functions for creating eye-catching and high-quality videos.

- You don't need to use third-party editing software when you want to publish something on the platform.

- Tiktok can be used as an affiliate marketing platform by inserting affiliate links in specific fields.

- For your future career path, you can consider TikTok as a portfolio for your videos. This can work well for those who desire to work in the graphics, animation, video editing, and digital media industry.

- This social media giant offers advanced algorithms that serve very relevant content to its users.

- Tiktok is a mobile app. Hence, promoted ads can be hard to block. This opportunity gives marketers the chance to garner 100% engagement with their promoted ads and ad campaigns.

- In terms of its user base, the platform has surpassed other social channels, including LinkedIn, Pinterest, and Snapchat.

- Tiktok is a great place for entertaining with humor and authenticity. Most of the viral videos on the platform are funny videos that are extremely funny.

Boasting more than 800 million active users, TikTok is definitely an ideal platform for organic marketing, brand promotion, and paid advertising. It also offers many opportunities for content creation and influencer and affiliate marketing.

Tiktok greatly caters to the younger generations belonging to the Generation Z and Generation Alpha. Although they don't have that much spending power, members from the said generations generate thousands of impressions and engagements. It will be great to start your social media career on TikTok. You can expand to other channels as your brand grows its followings.

TikTok offers not just funny cat videos and slapstick content. It's also a social channel that can help startups, freelancers, and entrepreneurs generate money through content creation and many forms of advertising.

Increasing TikTok Followers with Ease

- ☐ Publish contents that compliment your brand
- ☐ Use relevant and well-researched hashtags in your captions
- ☐ Follow TikTok trends
- ☐ Incorporate trending songs in your video clips
- ☐ Post videos during peak hours
- ☐ Join collaborations and niche events
- ☐ Partner with other content creators
- ☐ Use strong call-to-actions
- ☐ Post on a daily basis, but prioritize quality over quantity
- ☐ Gain new followers by following others
- ☐ Increase the number of your mutuals
- ☐ Comments on other videos
- ☐ Cross-promote your video clips on your other social channels

The Most Effective Ways to Make Money on TikTok: Becoming an Influencer, Selling TikTok

Accounts, and Many More!

According to Forbes, some TikTok influencers earn seven figures per month. Addison Rae Easterling, as an example, earned $5 million in 2020.

Over the years, social networks have become great income generators for many people. And that includes TikTok! In fact, HubSpot reported that TikTok is the fastest-growing social channel since 2019.

With its massive expansion, many marketing opportunities and earning ventures are becoming available to ordinary people. Even young children can earn on TikTok, just like on YouTube.

Now, here's the million-dollar question for you? How can you earn on TikTok? There are many ways, from making funny videos to being a member of TikTok's partnership programs. In addition to that, many of these legal money-making gigs cost zero dollars.

☐ **Becoming a TikTok Influencer**

On any social platform, influencers earn in two ways. They sell the products they get for free, and they receive payment by promoting brands, people, products, and services.

Once you've thousands of followers, you can become an influencer. Influencers are internet icons. They could have hundreds, thousands, or millions of followers. They provide entertainment or valuable insights, while focusing on their niches and industries.

Brands tend to partner with influencers because their promotions cost less than paid advertisements. On Instagram and TikTok, many entities prefer micro-influencers over those with 100,000 and above followers.

Micro-influencers could have 1,000 to 20,000 followers. Once a marketer contacts you, they'll request a promotion video coming from you. In exchange, they'll send you a product or two that you'll have to review in the video.

As simple as that, you could get a sports watch or even a brand-new Android phone for free! The more followers you have, the higher your earnings will be.

-How to Become an Influencer?

Here's a bonus section. Becoming a social media influencer may sound daunting, but in fact, all you need is a decent number of following and high engagement.

At this point, generating engagements could still be a puzzle for you. The step-by-step instructions below can help you land a promotion request. Promotion requests from brands allow influencers to earn on the platform.

1) Choose you niche

Choosing a niche is like selecting your very first Pokemon partner. You must choose from an assortment of different elements, and your choice should be compatible with your personality. In the world of influencer marketing, you've to choose from different niches and your preferences must be in line with your brand's voice.

For example, you're good at cooking and you're experienced in creating instructional videos. But you wish to cater to a gaming community despite not having that much gaming experience. Perhaps, you wish to receive a high-end smartphone. That's why you want to choose that niche.

However, how can you cater to your followers if you're a total noob naive? How can you understand the cultures and jargons surrounding the gaming industry? In the past, you may have had provided cooking videos. Hence, your current followers are the folks who've liked your previous TikTok videos.

Maybe, you don't even have a single follower who's into gaming. If you suddenly change the context of your videos in order to attract brands related to the gaming industry, only few people will "engage" with your content. Less engagement equals fewer views and impressions.

For influencers, engagement is everything. Even if you only have 1,500 followers but the number of engagements in your videos is higher than those who have 100,000 followers, your profile is valuable to marketers! Many will contact you!

So, what's the moral lesson here? You need to be an expert in your field. By focusing on a niche or two, you can impress the right audience and attract brands that you can really help. In case you wish to cater to a specific community, you must acquire first the necessary skills to thrive in their industry.

2) Setup your profile

Your bio and profile picture are two areas for consideration. They're very important! These are the fields that viewers will first see, once they watch a video clip from you. By all means, how you take advantage of them will decide whether or not your profile can garner followers at all.

In your bio, clearly state the purpose of your TikTok profile. You can also add some spice or personality to your message. Feel free to insert emojis and relevant quotes from famous people. Just remember that your bio needs to capture the hearts of prospects, in just one glance.

Regarding your profile picture, opt for an enticing and memorable image. Aside from your TikTok name, your fans should remember you once they see your profile picture. On the platform, it will serve as your emblem. Like your bio, it must also enthrall your audience.

3) Understand your audience

No two online communities are the same. So, your quirks, brand tone, and manner of handling conversations could be appealing to one group of people and annoying to another. Your styles and brand characteristics might irk others belonging to another group.

Working on your online persona requires likable content and communication style that your audience will love and relate to. Research your audience, create social media personas, and monitor what catches their attention. You must also know their preferences and the things that could annoy them.

4) Create unique and amazing contents

The last thing you should do on TikTok is to imitate everything that your rivals do. People on the web tend to frown upon plagiarism. If you do opt to publish a video that is very similar to someone, don't forget to credit the original.

On TikTok, quality videos that are engaging receives high engagement. Funny, creative, and entertaining videos have the potential to go viral. Viral content can bring in new followers. This could mean more engagements for your profile.

5) Stay relevant and be consistent

Like on other social platforms, such as Insta and Twitter, it's a necessity to post consistently and regularly on TikTok. According to SproutSocial, most of the top influencers on TikTok, like The Rock and Jojo Siwa, publish one to two videos per day.

Publish your content when most of your followers are likely active on the platform. You can uncover their schedules on the social channel by conducting social research.

6) Engage your audience and communicate with them

What's the secret of the top icons on social channels? They can communicate with their audience well, using their online contents, like visuals and videos. By responding to the sentiments of their followers, they form long-lasting bonds and strong relationships.

Whenever you answer an inquiry, respond to constructive criticism positively, and have a public chat with your followers, you're putting your brand under the spotlight.

And you're living a mark in the minds of your audience, especially to those you personally engage with.

As much as you can, reply to each praise and inquiry your followers make. Tell them that you're thankful for their comments. With words, always show gratitude. Most of all, make your followers feel special.

When it's their birthday, greet them! When they shared an accomplishment, tell them you're happy for them. If you think you're still not that close with the user, just say a simple word of congratulations. Follow this by an emoji.

Flabbergasting is frowned upon in the virtual world but exuding a bright and warm personality attracts people.

7) Declare that you're open to collaborations

This is the last step to becoming a TikTok influencer. Once you have a solid following, you can announce on your channel that you're accepting collaborations and partnerships. Sign up on platforms like Tomoson so that brands can find you easily.

On these websites, your follower counts across all of your social channels are added together. If a brand wants you to become an affiliate, then you'll have another source of income.

☐ **Growing and Selling TikTok Accounts**

When you have the magic formula to "increasing TikTok followers by the thousands," you can earn many, many bills of money. In fact, profiles with more than 5,000 followers can cost between $100 to

$150. Accounts with more than 20,000 followers are priced between $200 to $300.

This racket is already popular on Insta. TikTok users like Ramy Halloun earns between $20,000 to $30,000 yearly just by selling IG and TikTok accounts. In the following sections, you can learn how to grow your followers fast! FameSwap, a listings website, offers legit TikTok accounts that are up for grabs.

Once the profile has reached your target follower count, you can sell it on FameSwap and other similar websites. You have the option to specify the profile's category. In this field, you need to write the niches that the profile can cater to. This is important since you would be client needs engagement. So, the followers from the account being sold should be able to appreciate posts under the category you've listed.

☐ **Product Sales and Affiliate Commissions**

If you've high engagement, you can set up many income streams. You can create merchandise that you can sell or receive commissions from affiliate sales.

Just recently, TikTok has partnered with TeeSpring. With this partnership, TikTok content creators can sell merchandise under their name. Teespring allows you to monetize your brand and your creations.

If you created an icon or anything that you could use as a design, then you'll have your own merchandise. You can promote your products in your videos and sell them directly on the app.

With Teespring, you can customize a design for 180 different products. You don't need to worry about the materials. You just need to register on their website, submit your designs, and promote your stuff on social channels.

☐ **Promote a Brand or Business**

Audio sponsorships are not the only way to get paid with real money on TikTok. Both marketers and content creators can leverage their profiles to help brands have a successful launch. They can also aid in the promotion of new products.

Now, you won't be doing that for free. Marketers, brand owners, and companies will pay you for the promotional content you'll make for them.

Your advertising services will be paid for. One example is the partnership between Mucinex and many top TikTok influencers. The company launched the branded hashtag #BeatTheZombieFunk and made it viral with the help of some internet icons, like OurFire.

Creators who desire to have brand sponsorships should reach out to businesses and brands. They can also find opportunities through Tiktok's Creator Marketplace.

☐ **Get Paid by TikTok**

Like YouTube, TikTok also pays its top content creators who meet certain criteria. The social giant said, "We want to help our creators and make them earn solely on the platform."

In 2020, TikTok launched a $200 million creator's fund, and they plan to increase the amount to $1 billion by 2023. With this program, TikTok pays channel owners for making videos. Payments are wired to their bank accounts, transferred to PayPal, or sent through Western Union.

It functions much like YouTube's partnership program. To qualify, you need at least 10,000 followers and garner 10,000 views in 30 days. If you wish to join the program, you can apply through your TikTok profile. In the notification section on the app, you'll receive an application invitation. TikTok will invite you directly if you meet the requirements.

☐ **Converting Gifts to Diamonds**

This is perhaps the most popular way to earn money on TikTok, and it's also the easiest one. Now, how can you get gifts? And how can you convert diamonds to money? Of course, these are not real diamonds. So, in one way or another, you need to turn them into cold, hard cash.

When you host live streams, your viewers can send you gifts. These gifts are purchased with virtual coins that can be bought on TikTok. Creators can then convert the gifts into "diamonds."

Diamonds are TikTok's virtual credits. You can cash out your credits into real money, through many ways, like PayPal and wire transfer. You need to be at least 18 years old to withdraw diamonds. For underage streamers, they transfer their money to a relative's account. By doing this, they can bypass TikTok's age restrictions.

Chapter Conclusion

TikTok is just a fairly new social platform, but it has great potential. In just three years, it has grown from a small streaming app to a social media giant. If you choose to include TikTok into your SMM strategy, it will be a valuable tool for your brand's growth. The app emphasizes on niche-focused contents. That's why budding profiles have a high chance for growth on this platform. If you're looking for another fairly new social network that is similar to TikTok, then your brand could benefit from Twitch's free services as well.

CHAPTER 7: THE ULTIMATE GUIDE TO TWITCH MARKETING

Today, Twitch is the world's largest video game streaming platform aside from being one of the top ten largest social channels on the web. In February 2021, the website experienced approximately 25 million active users. On average, 3.1 billion minutes are watched per day.

Streamers on Twitch need to only find their niche and be exposed to their target audience, in order to earn on the platform. Once this is met, you can make money through different ways, from streaming Esports matches to promoting affiliate products. This is also referred to as "sponsorship," which includes commission sales.

In this chapter, you can learn how to market anything on Twitch. You'll also be able to make more sales, generate more leads, and expand your brand's reach.

Twitch is a social networking website, on top of being a live streaming platform. It's the best place to stream Esports competitions. Its user base is predominantly made up of gamers. Nevertheless, Twitch is slowly becoming more than it has been designed to be. Since 2019, DIY, music, creative, and lifestyle niches have been growing.

The Statistics

Based on the statistics below, Twitch is the number one live streaming platform. It accounts for 72% of all live-streamed hours watched on the web. If you're still hesitant of branding on Twitch, check out the facts below. They could convince you.

- In February 2021, there were 2.9 million average concurrent Twitch viewers.
- Ninja is the most-followed user on the platform, as of March 2021.
- All-time, the most-viewed channel is Fextralife, who is also known as SocialBlade.
- 41% of Twitch's userbase is comprised of Gen Z's and 32% are Millennials.
- Approximately 26 million people visit the platform daily.
- 90 billion minutes are watched per month.

In the following sections, you'll know whether or not this platform is right for you and your brand. Today, many top marketers, like GoldGlove and Sodapoppin, are speculating that Twitch could be the next TikTok. TikTok was originally just a lip-syncing and dance video recording platform. Now, it has become one of the top multi-purpose platforms.

Knowing More About Twitch Influencer Marketing

This is similar to the other form of influencer marketing discussed in the previous sections. However, there's an exception. Promotional content or the infomercial for the sponsor is live streamed. This is in contrast to the conventional use of images and prerecorded videos.

Marketers and brand representatives reach out to streamers for the purpose of negotiating partnerships and promotion details. Some deals involve the signing of contracts. Some just send products in exchange for a mention or a Livestream demo.

Once an agreement is reached, the streamer will promote the brand on a specific date. The date and time of streaming could also be based on the contract. On this kind of social platform, many forms of promotions exist. The most common are demos, giveaways, shout-outs, and product unboxing.

In fact, you can introduce your own kind of promotion. Do you want it to be funny or educational? It's up to you. Promotions of products and services related to the game you're streaming work well with audiences. For example, some DOTA players will love to have their own DOTA 2-themed shirts.

Don't forget to conduct giveaways. Influencers will end up having excess merchandise from their sponsors. If you have a good number following, you can ask for multiple products for future giveaways.

How Twitch Works

As mentioned earlier, most of the viewers and streamers on the platform are for video game content. Much like YouTube live streamers, registered Twitch users talk and engage their viewers while playing games live. They can also chat in real-time.

Within the gaming industry, several niche markets exist. For example, first-person shooting (FPS) streams are mainly viewed by Fortnite and Valorant players. MOBA [will add abbreviation of this] games popular on Twitch are DOTA 2, Smite, Mobile Legends, and League of Legends (LOL). MMORPGs is making a comeback since 2020, with Genshin Impact's launch and MH World's release.

Hence, before you choose what to stream, research first if there are a lot of viewers of that game. You must know whether or not it's currently trendy on the platform.

Twitch viewers watch streams for a variety of reasons. These demands can be categorized into three:

1) Streamers are highly skilled at their chosen game

2) Some live streamers have very engaging personalities. They could be funny or quirky, in a positive way.

3) Streamers have excellent personalities and tons of skills.

Using Twitch for Marketing

In 2017, Statistica reported that Twitch users are 80% males and 55% of the whole user base are between 16 to 34 years old. But, in 2019, the total number of female Twitch users increased by 15%.

Their massive user base dedicated to particular niches has brought forth many advertising opportunities. Tech companies, eCommerce brands, and apparel manufacturers have entered the platform, in order to collaborate with the top icons.

Even YouTubers are harnessing the potential of Twitch streamers. They pay fees and offer free products for mentions, partnerships, and promotions. Ninja and Shroud are just some examples.

The best part about Twitch is its targeted content. Most content creators on the platform focus on only one or two genres or game franchises. It's kind of rare to see their top icons play multiple game types. For example, MrBallen [How many subscribers does he have?] only focuses on retro games, like Donkey Kong and Mario.

Ninja and SocialBlade are some of the exceptions. They stream various content across different gaming consoles. There's a wealth of benefits by opting for their style. Many brands will be interested in collaborating with you. Top influencers on Twitch receive free gaming consoles from industry giants, like Nintendo, Sony, Acer, and Microsoft.

Like on other social platforms, now is the right time to start on Twitch. Don't wait when the markets become more and more saturated. And avoid streaming without a marketing plan. You'll just be wasting your time. Before you create content on Twitch, build your audience first and engage with like-minded individuals. To get started, please follow the guide below:

1) Set your marketing goals. You need objectives, and you need goals. Along the way, these might change. But it's best to write them down first before you proceed to the next phases. Then your list in this step can guide you as you fulfill the other instructions.

2) Understand your target audience. Know their pain points and what they seek from streamers.

3) Whether you already have a sponsor or you want to promote something, save the advertisement after you've entertained your audience.

4) Develop a unique identity that will allow your viewers to differentiate you from the rest. This could be a unique quirk or personality, a notable appearance, or a catchphrase like "ladies and gentlemen."

5) Study the tactics of your fellow influencers. Watch how they stream and how they engage their viewers. In your niche, what kind of content has the greatest number of views? You must find the answer to this question.

6) Once you're done researching viewers and competitors, list down the important stuff and revise your marketing goals accordingly.

7) You need a marketing calendar. In this stage, the schedule of most of your viewers should be known to you. With this knowledge, you can know when the best time is to post and at what days of the week, they're most active.

8) Consider viewer sentiment and interact with your audience. An active and positive community is the best place to start. In case you choose a niche where toxic behavior is rampant, you must be a breath of fresh air to the players. Ignore trolls and haters. Instead, always positively respond to questions, greetings, fan messages, and constructive criticisms. You can chat with them using the message field or answer them in real-time.

-Sample Scenario

One reason that Twitch users watch live game streams is to learn. They could be seeking strategies and game tricks or information about how to defeat the latest boss. Avid gamers also watch game news and interpretation of updates.

While being friendly and exuding an excellent personality, treat your viewers as students. They watch you because they want something from you. Aside from entertaining them, provide valuable gaming tips and tricks.

In online games, newly introduced bosses can be hard to vanquish and tier resets make it hard for players to upgrade their ranks. So, after an update, players will be seeking information about the easiest ways to beat the boss. They will want to get their hands on the best loots, which require specific achievements to be unlocked.

For example, 7DS: Grand Cross, a game adaptation of the popular Seven Deadly Sins anime, has a growing community on Twitch. Nowadays, it's very popular among anime enthusiasts and RPG gamers. It features fast-paced 3D action and high-quality cinematics and action-pack gameplay.

Now, the bosses on Grand Cross's Death Match mode are very hard to defeat. You can't clear the higher stages if you just use random characters. To defeat Belmos and The Silver Demon, you need heroes with speed affinities. Not only that, but you can also only the specific stages by using particular heroes and by following a particular strategy. If you fight head-on, your team will just be obliterated in the second or third round.

As a content creator of the game, you need to provide solutions to those pain points. Stream your next boss raid. Show your viewers the required team for clearing the stage. Explain what gear they should use. As you progress through every round, tell them what needs to be done to defeat the boss and garner the highest points.

You must be a regular provider of such solutions in your niche so that more and more people will recognize you and subscribe to your channel. You can earn legit money on Twitch through various ways if you have thousands of subscribers.

The Best Tips and Tricks to Increase Subscriber Count

Once you've fulfilled the steps in the previous sections, the next thing you need to do on Twitch is to grow your following. You need targeted and dedicated viewers, in order to earn and grow your channel. With the tips below, catch the hearts of active users and entice them to become your regular viewers, succinctly.

- ☐ Engage with other influencers
- ☐ Network your brand
- ☐ Interact with your target audience and provide valuable information
- ☐ Promote your Twitch channel on your other social media timelines
- ☐ Join Facebook groups and build your reputation there
- ☐ Don't be ashamed to ask for subscribers on Instagram and Facebook

- ☐ Implement an effective and eye-catching Twitch layout
- ☐ Be good at your game
- ☐ Join events and meetups near your region
- ☐ Interact with people there and exchange follows
- ☐ Launch a paid campaign
- ☐ Collaborate with other contents creators
- ☐ Follow accounts that offer free *follows*
- ☐ Provide high-quality streaming and clear sounds
- ☐ Interact with your viewers using a headphone and receiver
- ☐ Use hashtags and keywords in your stream descriptions
- ☐ Save gameplays and video clips to your profile and make them public
- ☐ Contribute valuable content on Twitch forums on Reddit, GameFaqs, etc.
- ☐ Upload Twitch stream highlights on YouTube and TikTok
- ☐ Always ask for subs and likes in your posts and videos
- ☐ Exude a friendly and wonderful personality overall

Leveraging Twitch Marketing

Given the facts, Twitch is indeed an excellent marketing platform for businesses related to the gaming and tech industry. It generates much engagement, and many are also using it to grow their other social channels. And, since it's a pretty new platform right now, it will be easier to shine on Twitch than on other social platforms.

Here are four ways you can use Twitch for branding:

- Improving Brand Awareness

Twitch provides unique opportunities to engage with prospects. Recently, they collaborated with the 1,000 Dreams Fund. This partnership has provided opportunities for female streamers still studying in college.

Cross-pollination of content highlighted the grant on social media. In 2018 TwitchCon, Doritos partnered with Twitch and did something similar.

- Influencer Marketing

Twitch focuses on community and connection building, making a good platform for both affiliate and influencer marketing. Collaborating with a popular streamer can expose your own brand to thousands of new people.

You may give up a few hundred bucks for your preferred influencer, but with this move, you can earn more than ten-fold of your investment. Big brands have already engaged in influencer marketing. Why shouldn't you?

On Twitch, KFC partnered with streamers Sacriel, Dr.Lupo, and many more. They created the #ChickenDinnerChallenge, which have probably enticed to order KFC fried chicken buckets since the promotional streams were mouth-watering.

- Lead Generation

Like other social channels, Twitch can help you generate leads for your website or other online profiles. You can even use it to feature your LinkedIn In.

Both Wendy's and Head & Shoulders have successfully done that. With Twitch and its top streamers, both brands have increased sales. Wendy's has taken one step further. They partnered with Fortnite players and created their own channel on the platform.

They created a branded hashtag on Twitch. Wendy's freezer destroying campaign garnered almost 2 million views and generate a 119% increase in mentions across other social channels.

- Paid Media

Like YouTube, Twitch plays video advertisements. The ads often pop up before and after streams. By signing up on pre-roll ads, you can improve your brand's exposure.

Both paid advertising and organic marketing on Twitch expose brands to targeted audiences. With pre-roll ads, you can opt to have it only ran during streams of specific games.

For example, indeed utilized Twitch's paid ads to connect streamers and talents with a campaign. This ad campaign is designed to showcase the aim of the entity. Indeed, is a career search engine, similar to LinkedIn.

Since there's a growing community that embraces self-improvement videos on Twitch, indeed has taken advantage of that growing market. They use Twitch to generate leads and improve brand awareness. Many streamers also started seeking talents on their platform.

Should You Use Twitch for Your Brand?

Many marketers shy away from Twitch. They ask themselves should they invest their time and effort in this marketing platform. Nevertheless, it's evident that the brands that have taken the risk experienced profitable results. If your brand caters to Millennials and younger audiences who are into the major niches thriving on the platform, then why not give Twitch marketing a try?

CONCLUSION

I'd like to thank you and congratulate you for transiting my lines from start to finish. I hope this book was able to help you to learn everything you need to know about social media marketing.

The next step is to create your social channels, conduct both customer and competitor research, formulate your marketing plan, and launch your brand on the top social networking platforms out there.

I wish you the best of luck!

www.ingramcontent.com/pod-product-compliance
Lightning Source LLC
Chambersburg PA
CBHW062102220526
45471CB00010B/3573